THE ESSENCE OF
JUNG'S PSYCHOLOGY
& TIBETAN BUDDHISM

THE ESSENCE OF
JUNG'S PSYCHOLOGY
AND TIBETAN BUDDHISM

Western and Eastern Paths to the Heart

Radmila Moacanin

Wisdom Publications • Boston

Wisdom Publications
199 Elm Street
Somerville MA 02144 USA
www.wisdompubs.org

Library of Congress Cataloging-in-Publication Data
Moacanin, Radmila
    The essence of Jung's psychology and Tibetan Buddhism :
  western and eastern paths to the heart / Radmila Moacanin
       p. cm.
Originally published: Jung's psychology and Tibetan Buddhism.
  London : Wisdom, 1986.
Includes biblioraphical references and index.
    ISBN 0-86171-340-0 (pbk. : alk. paper)
    1. Buddhism—Psychology. 2. Jung, C. G. (Carl Gustav),
  1875–1961. 3. Buddhism—China—Tibet. I. Title
BQ4570.P76 M63 2003
294.3/375—dc21   2002155427

07 06 05 04 03
5 4 3 2

Interior design by Gopa & Ted2

Wisdom Publications' books are printed on acid-free paper and meet the
guidelines for permanence and durability of the Committee on Production
Guidelines for Book Longevity of the Council on Library Resources.

Printed in Canada

Contents

Preface to
the Second Edition

If some great idea takes hold of us from outside,
we must understand that it takes hold of us
only because something in us responds to it,
and goes out to meet it.
—C. G. Jung

Since this book was first published much has happened in our world that makes the teachings of Tibetan Buddhism and the work of Jung even more relevant. The past century ended and the new one was ushered in with an explosion of violence, indiscriminate killing, and revenge: the eye-for-an-eye attitude that—as Gandhi said—leads to a blind world. In addition, our planet, the only habitat we have, one that we share with all other living beings, has been deeply wounded: earth, water, and air have been poisoned by mindless exploitation and by man-made instruments of destruction, all in pursuit of power and self-centered interests.

In the last decade or so we have seen enormous and increasingly accelerated advances in technology with relatively few advances in the spiritual realm. Militarism, materialism, and consumerism have run amok to the point of drowning Western civilization and rapidly infecting the rest of humanity. Together they emphasize the external and disregard the inner world. As a result our world is not only blind but unconscious and asleep.

There are, however, some signs in Western culture—albeit a minority subculture—of a slowly emerging trend, a paradigm

shift beyond scientific materialism to greater self-awareness and
mental receptivity; to interest in meditation and the intersection
of psychology and spirituality; to examining one's values and
simplifying one's life, including career changes, for a more ful-
filling existence; in brief, there is a trend away from *Logos*—the
pure intellect that analyzes, judges, and divides—to *Eros,* which
relates and connects, and brings the realization of our intercon-
nectedness and interdependence. This shift touches our depths,
opening us to larger dimensions, to the ineffable mystery of life
and death, and leading us to the spiritual transformation that
Tibetan Buddhism and the work of Jung are all about.

The mere fact that this book has gone through three printings
and two editions and has been translated into eleven languages
shows that there is a hunger for the perennial wisdom of East
and West as eloquently expressed both by Tibetan Buddhism and
by Jung.

Tibetan Buddhism has become relatively well known, especially since 1989 when the Dalai Lama was awarded the Nobel
Peace Prize. Today he is regarded by many as the world's greatest and most inspiring religious leader, thanks to his unwavering
commitment to nonviolence, his unconditional respect for human
life, and his reverence for all living beings and the environment
within which they live. Jung, however, is still not properly understood, and his vital contributions have not been fully recognized
even by Western psychology.

This second edition includes an epilogue in which I explore
a few of the most significant topics at the intersection of Jung's
psychology and Tibetan Buddhism, with special emphasis on
their relevance to our present world.

Preface

This book had its origins in Europe, when some years ago the Tibetan Buddhist master, Lama Thubten Yeshe, flew West from Asia to give teachings, and I flew East from America to receive them. One day in a private interview with him, knowing of my interest in Jung, he asked me unexpectedly to give a talk on Jung's psychology and its relation to Tibetan Buddhism. I protested: I was totally unprepared and knew so little about it. But Lama gently insisted. Frightened, I kept pleading with him to be excused from such an impossible task, but he was relentless and would not hear of it. For the first and only time in my acquaintance with Lama Yeshe, I truly believed we had failed to communicate. Little did I know what was to follow.

Later that very same day I quietly sat cross-legged on the floor of the meditation room in front of a large audience of Lama Yeshe's students and proceeded to deliver the talk. It turned out to be a memorable and a major event in my life. From then on I was gripped by the urge to learn and experience more of the two traditions. I began traveling on that exciting journey East and West, West and East, and in my mind, each of the two disciplines supplemented, helped explain further, and enriched the other. As a result, a few years later this book was produced. Synchronistically, just as it came into being in California, Lama Yeshe arrived there after a long absence. I showed him the work, and he immediately encouraged me to have it published. Once again I was reluctant, but once again it was a task from which I could not be excused.

The book attempts to draw parallels, and discuss similarities and differences, between Tibetan Buddhism and Jung's psychology. The purpose is to identify possible connections so as to make a bridge between some aspects of Eastern and Western philosophical and spiritual traditions, psychological and ethical systems.

One of the main problems I want to investigate is the following: since the two traditions have developed at different historical times, under vastly different sociocultural conditions and geographically at two opposite sides of the world, are they intrinsically discrete and of psychological and ethical value only to the people where each developed? Or is it possible to reconcile the two traditions, "bring the twain together," allow a cross-fertilization, synthesize and adapt the findings, methods, and wisdom of the respective systems to the needs and conditions of contemporary society, regardless of geographical boundaries?

Other related questions that I will put forward for investigation are as follows. Are there possible dangers inherent in allowing the Westerner to experiment with long-established and deeply rooted Eastern traditions? Are those dangers due basically to transplantation of spiritual discipline from one culture to another—from East to West—in the way the reverse occurred when Western industrial technology was introduced in so-called underdeveloped countries of the East, causing disruption of traditional patterns of living and working and consequently often serious damage to the psychological equilibrium of the individuals concerned? Or are the dangers even more fundamental, like those the alchemists knew and warned us about—that their *opus* was "like a death-dealing poison," meaning not only hazards of chemical poisoning but also of mental aberrations. What then are the necessary precautions and safeguards, if any, in approaching the studies and practices of an Eastern spiritual discipline that has been kept secret for centuries and has only recently been revealed to the Western world?

C. G. Jung, the alchemists, and Tibetan Buddhists, have they all been in search of the same truth—Self, Philosopher's Stone, enlightenment? Have their works a common core that, if properly understood and practiced, contains a universal value?

Is there a meaningful coincidence in the eighth-century prophecy that "when the iron birds will fly the Tibetans will leave their home," the prophecy being fulfilled in the very twentieth century that brought C. G. Jung to us?

Many Tibetans have found a new home in Switzerland, one of the most congenial places for them outside of Tibet, viewing the same Alps that inspired Jung and that are reminiscent of their own Himalayas, surroundings and visions particularly conducive for the mind to meditate and expand.

Some years back, under the impact of the very same force that made the Tibetans leave their home, I too had to leave mine, and found temporarily a new home in Switzerland. It was there that my first interest in Eastern mystical traditions was born. It was in Switzerland also that I had my first encounter with the Dalai Lama. Since meeting Tibetan lamas, I have often felt grateful, in a strange way, to that "evil" force that was directly instrumental in bringing us together. For me this represented a striking example of the possibility of experiencing that "thought transformation" that the Tibetans teach, and a demonstration of the multidimensional aspects of every event.

I came into contact both with the work of Jung and with Tibetan Buddhism very spontaneously, and in each case as the result of a series of synchronistic events. Both systems had an immediate and strong impact on me, and I had an intimation that somehow they must be related in a profoundly significant way, despite the fact that they were rooted in different traditions and developed under different outward circumstances.

In this book I shall try to encompass general areas of Jung's psychology and Tibetan Buddhism. These are subject matters of immense scope and complexity, in both theory and practice, and voluminous works have been produced in each of the areas. Therefore my study shall be limited to only certain issues dealt with by Jung, and the relation of alchemy to his own findings.

The discussion of Buddhism will focus on tantric Buddhism and its relation to Jung's psychology. I can hardly discuss tantric Buddhism, however, without placing it in the broader context of Tibetan Buddhism in general. This is the rationale for giving a brief overview of Tibetan Buddhism. The rationale for discussing tantric Buddhism and relating it to Jung's psychology is based on my impression that this particular form of Buddhism is most directly concerned with the issues and problems that preoccupied Jung throughout his life—above all, the process of the growth of consciousness and spiritual transformation. Jung refers to it as "the tremendous experiment of becoming conscious, which nature has laid upon mankind, and which unites the most diverse cultures in a common task."

Despite its intricate complexity and esoteric nature, Tibetan Buddhism is essentially a psychological and ethical system. And unlike other philosophical theories and spiritual approaches that have come to us from Asia, tantric Buddhism is very much a living process, bridging the gap between our deepest yearnings for symbolic and spiritual mystery, and the demands of our mundane life, always stressing that the meaning of life is in living it.

I hope to arrive at some solutions to a few fundamental issues examined, and that the results will demonstrate and point to interconnections between the two systems. I hope to be able to show that it is possible to reconcile an ancient Eastern spiritual discipline with a contemporary Western psychological system in a fruitful and meaningful way.

Acknowledgments

My profound gratitude and heartfelt thanks to my teachers, Lama Thubten Yeshe and Lama Thubten Zopa Rinpoche, who showed me the path to another reality; to Dr. Ira Progoff, who introduced me to the world of Jung; to Dr. Russell Lockhart: with his guidance the horizons of that multidimensional world expanded beyond all boundaries; to my mother, who patiently gave me invaluable help and support; to many friends and strangers in Europe and Asia, the Americas, Africa, and Australia, who with their hearts and minds contributed to this work in many different ways.

1 *Buddhism*

Once upon a time, in a far-off land there was a prince who had a beautiful wife and a young son. He was called Siddhartha Gautama. He had lived all his life in a big palace and according to his father's wishes never left the palace. His father, the king, was determined to protect his son and heir from seeing any misery and to offer him all the worldly pleasures of life. Indeed, Siddhartha tasted to the full all the worldly pleasures of life.

But one day he disobeyed his father's strict orders never to leave the palace grounds. With his devoted companion and charioteer Channa, he passed beyond the gate and ventured into the world. He came across an old man, a sick man, and a dead man—three sights totally unknown to the young prince. He asked Channa whether he ever saw anything like that. Channa answered that old age, sickness, and death must come to all of us. For the first time in his life, Siddhartha was wounded by the arrow of a new awareness: the suffering of all humanity from which there is no escape. Finally, the fourth and decisive sight Siddhartha encountered was that of a wandering holy man. He no longer had a choice: the inner urgency, his newly discovered calling, was overwhelming, and he too had to leave his home, his royal life, and everything he cherished, including his parents, his beautiful wife, and small son.

Silently he left the royal palace for good to embark alone on a long journey in pursuit of answers to the riddle of life. In his wanderings he met many famous learned teachers and philosophers; he studied with them and followed their methods. But none of the learned men could answer his own questions, for these were no ordinary questions, not formulated in his head, but felt deeply in his heart, searching not for philosophical and metaphysical speculations but the living truth. So, Siddhartha continued his solitary journey searching for his treasure, the only treasure he so desperately wanted, and for which he was determined once more to sacrifice everything.

For many years he lived in the forest as a hermit endeavoring to gain control over his body and his mind. He was successful in his efforts, but the results were a starved, extremely weakened body and a discouraged mind, while the treasure he was seeking still eluded him. At the depth of hopelessness Siddhartha realized that his body was his most precious instrument, not to be abused through ascetic practices any more than through sense indulgence, both of which he had known so well. It was through his human body—and through it alone—that he could reach the treasure hard to find. Now it was time for the former prince and the former ascetic to change his life again, to abandon the way of self-denial and enter a more balanced path—the Middle Path. So, he took a meal, bathed, put on fresh clothes. Siddhartha then sat cross-legged under a tree to meditate and vowed not to remove himself from this spot till he found the treasure. And indeed after many days of sitting under the tree the treasure came to him: in a flash of illumination he attained enlightenment, the living truth he had been searching for. At that moment Siddhartha became the Buddha, the Awakened One.

He lived a long life bringing the treasure he discovered to many people, young and old, rich and poor, learned and uneducated, to everyone and anyone who was ready to discover the treasure for himself; for the treasure was to be found nowhere else but within the depth of each individual mind. His mortal body died at the age of eighty or so. But Prince Siddhartha Gautama—the Buddha—lived happily ever after in the minds and hearts of millions of human beings who accepted his message and made it a living reality.

This is the tale of Shakyamuni Buddha, probably one of the oldest, most often repeated, most fantastic of all tales. It has been told and has inspired countless human beings for two and a half millennia.

What was the message that Shakyamuni Buddha brought to the world? Above all that each human being has the potential to attain enlightenment and become a buddha. "Man is his own master, and there is no higher being or power that sits in judgment over his destiny."[1] Buddha, and his followers to this day, can only teach, guide, point to the path to liberation; each person must enter and walk the path alone, just as Siddhartha did. One must maintain a healthy doubt about the teachings one receives, no matter who the authority, including the Buddha, until their validity is clearly confirmed through investigation, analysis, and experience. Only when we have discovered that the teachings are valuable and applicable to our own life should we follow them. Ultimately, we are our own authority in the spiritual quest; there is no revealed truth, sacred scripture, no dogma and no savior.

The essence of Buddha's teaching and the foundation of all subsequent Buddhist doctrine was expressed in his first sermon delivered at Sarnath, near Benares, after his enlightenment on the night of the full moon of July. In it he expounded the four noble truths:

1. suffering in life is ubiquitous;
2. the source of suffering is to be found in selfish craving and attachment of all kinds;
3. cessation, liberation, freedom from suffering is possible;
4. the path leading from suffering to liberation.

The four noble truths doctrine further elaborates on this path, generally referred to as the Middle Way because it is free from all extremes. It is also called the noble eightfold path as it specifies rules of behavior, in thought, speech, and action that lead to liberation. They are:

1. right understanding
2. right thought—purpose or aspiration
3. right speech
4. right action
5. right livelihood
6. right effort
7. right mindfulness, awareness, attentiveness
8. right concentration, or meditation

These eight categories constitute the foundations of Buddhist training, which when properly applied and followed lead to a balanced and harmonious life, benefiting both individual and society. The first two categories—right understanding and right thought—have to do with development of wisdom; the next three—right speech, right action, and right livelihood—with ethical conduct; and the last two—right mindfulness, and right concentration—with mental discipline.

Wisdom, ethical conduct, and mental discipline are interrelated and are to be pursued simultaneously, each promoting the development of the other. Thus the philosophical, ethical, and psychological components together constitute the foundation for spiritual development.[2]

In the subsequent centuries, from this simple yet very profound exposition of the four noble truths and the noble eightfold path pronounced by Shakyamuni Buddha, a staggering amount of interpretations through oral commentaries and written material evolved, often contradictory and conflicting. Some deal with plain practical issues, some with highly philosophical, metaphysical, and ontological problems, but they all claim to derive their authority from the utterances of Buddha himself. And indeed they are all variations on the same basic theme contained in the four noble truths, Buddha's first sermon. Furthermore the origin of the different and often controversial aspects of the doctrine is to be found in the very approach Shakyamuni Buddha used in his teachings, the only aim of which was to show human beings the way to emancipation from suffering, that is, liberation. Since suffering is a basic fact of life, the goal is common to all but the roads to its elimination are many. To quote the view on this issue of a contemporary Tibetan lama:

> A major characteristic of all Buddha's teachings is that they are designed to fit the needs and aptitudes of each individual. Since we all have different interests, problems, and ways of life, no one method of instruction could ever be suitable for everyone. Buddha himself explained that for the purpose of reaching a particular disciple coming from a particular background, he would teach a particular doctrine. Thus there could be certain times when it might be necessary to say "yes" and others when it would be more appropriate to say "no," even in response to the same question.[3]

This precisely is the strength of Buddhism, namely the flexibility of its methods and practice, its emphasis on each individual's experience, not intellectual, philosophical knowledge alone, or blind faith. Nothing, no method is excluded that could lead to the ultimate goal of liberation. This endows the teachings with an exquisite ability to adapt to the conditions of various people, living in different geographical climates, different cultures, and from different historical backgrounds. In this sense Buddhism has truly a universal character, and a relevance to life, that has persisted undiminished to this day, for its wisdom is rooted in the depth of the human psyche.

With such a wide latitude in matters of instruction and practice, it was inevitable that during the ensuing centuries after Buddha's death doctrinal differences would emerge and a variety of traditions would develop. Two major systems arose: what is sometimes called the *Hinayana*, literally, the "Lesser Vehicle," and the *Mahayana*, the "Greater Vehicle." The former developed into the Buddhism now practiced in Burma, Thailand, and Sri

Lanka, while the latter spread to what is now northern India, Mongolia, Tibet, Sikkim, Bhutan, Nepal, Cambodia, Vietnam, China, Korea, and Japan.

The Hinayana stresses strict moral regulations and adherence to austere vows of conduct. The ultimate goal is attainment of one's own salvation. The highest stage of individual development, the ideal human being, is called an "arhat." The word means "a slayer of the foe," and the foe is understood to be the passions.[4]

The Mahayana continues where Hinayana leaves off: the ultimate goal of Mahayanists is to seek salvation not for their own sake but for the benefit of all beings. And this goal is no less than the attainment of buddhahood. While Hinayana emphasizes austerity, self-restraint, and high ethical behavior, Mahayana emphasizes intuitive wisdom to remove the veil of ignorance obscuring our pure essence, the buddha nature dwelling in all of us and which only needs to be uncovered. To find one's true self, realize oneself, is to realize the inherent buddha nature. It has been said that "[Hinayana] emphasizes the humanity of the Buddha; Mahayana emphasizes the buddha nature of humanity."[5]

The ideal of the arhat in Hinayana is replaced in the Mahayana system by the ideal of the bodhisattva. From the ideal of a purely private salvation of arhats intent upon realizing nirvana, bodhisattvas have vowed to devote all their pursuits to the welfare of others and to work for a universal deliverance of all beings. In them any self-seeking, egoistic actions and endeavors are totally absent.

> Gentle and not abusive,
> Without deceit and fraud,
> Full of love towards all beings—
> So is a Bodhisattva.[6]

The word *bodhisattva* has been defined as meaning "heroic being," "spiritual warrior," or "illumined heart and valiant one."[7]

Bodhisattvas, "gentle and not abusive," react spontaneously to their impulse of compassion toward everyone and all, and are fully involved in the affairs of the world; they are in the midst of it, with all its struggles and tribulations. Theirs is not a negative way of denying and abandoning the world, but a positive way of affirming it and transforming it, by virtue of their great compassion and great wisdom. Their life task is to set people free from ignorance, passion, and evil.

Bodhisattvas have made the indestructible resolution to become a buddha solely for the benefit of others; they have thus single-mindedly entered and are pursuing the way of the enlightened being to become fully integrated, free from confusion and inner conflict. They have developed the means to tap the inner treasure of others, the latent seeds of enlightenment, which according to Mahayana is the common heritage of humanity. They are "...like the skillful alchemist who by virtue of the power of his chemicals can change silver into gold and gold into silver."[8]

One naturally wonders and asks:

> What is it that gives the bodhisattva this strength by which he excels all the rest? It is his capacity to sustain the comprehension of the true nature of things, his capacity to bear with every circumstance devoid of fear and anxiety, and his ability to meet every situation with unimpeded insight and unbounded compassion.[9]

I have frequently asked myself that same question while in the presence of Tibetan lamas, some of whom, I have not the slightest doubt, have attained the stage of a bodhisattva. And I have also wondered over the exquisite ability with which they are capable of affecting the minds and lives of many Westerners whose historical and cultural background and lifestyles are so vastly different from those of people born and raised in Tibet. Perhaps part of the answer lies in the following description of the bodhisattva:

From the very outset he seeks to realize the wisdom that constitutes Buddhahood, viz., the knowledge of all forms, the knowledge of all the ways of all beings. This is what gives the Buddhas and the advanced bodhisattvas the ability to keep themselves *en rapport* with every situation and render help to each individual in the way suited to him.[10]

Tibetan Buddhism

Tibetan Buddhism is part of the Mahayana. When it was introduced into Tibet from India in the seventh century A.D., it met with the native Bon religion and its shamanic practices. As Buddhism spread, many Indian scholars came to Tibet and translated religious texts and their commentaries until Tibetans themselves began writing their own commentaries. It has been said that on the Tibetan soil, Buddhism mixed with the local Bon cult and incorporated some of its features. The present Dalai Lama, however, denies any extraneous influences and states that "the Buddhist teaching that spread to Tibet is just the stainless teaching of India and nothing else. The Tibetan lamas neither altered it nor mixed it with another religion."[11]

In the course of time four major schools arose: the *Nyingma, Kargyu, Sakya,* and *Gelug.* Each of these schools traces its lineage to different Indian scholars and consequently presents variations in the mode of instructions, but Tibetans emphasize that there are no fundamental differences in their philosophy and spiritual practices. All are in quest of the same goal: enlightenment. In fact all adhere to the teachings of both Hinayana and Mahayana, and also Tantrayana (a division of Mahayana). *Yana* is the Sanskrit word for vehicle. A contemporary lama, in one of his lectures, equated this vehicle to a path or an elevator to lift up our consciousness to enlightenment.

There are three principal aspects of that path to enlightenment, the spiritual journey: renunciation, the enlightened motive, and the correct view of reality. "Blended together they are like the fuel propelling our rocket to the moon of enlightenment."[12] I shall now try to outline them very briefly.

Before entering the path, individuals in all their actions are motivated only by egocentric desires to acquire wealth, power, reputation, i.e., to have pleasure and escape from pain. But little do they know that the scramble for wealth, power, and any worldly aim can never bring satisfaction. This pursuit is what Buddhists call the condition of *samsara*—a Sanskrit term that means "circling." In this life it refers to our ingrained strong habit of going around and around in circles, chasing after gratification of desires, pleasures of one sort or another, which are invariably eluding us. This is the *perpetuum mobile* of mundane life: moving from one situation to another, fluctuating from one mood to another, desiring an object, acquiring and tasting it, becoming saturated, frustrated, discarding it, and turning around to start the very same process again and again. We never reach the sought-after goal, for the very characteristic of samsara is dissatisfaction—suffering. The term *samsara* applies also to the cyclic existence of continuous rebirths, out of which there is no escape, until liberation, that is, nirvana. In that sense *samsara* means "the round of existence."

According to Buddhist thought the source of samsara is ignorance, that is, unawareness, going about in response to the promptings of hedonistic impulses, an unconscious, undisciplined, uncontrolled, scattered mind.[13]

Another kind of ignorance is our delusion that phenomena are permanent, whereas impermanence, change, is the ubiquitous law of nature. We are attached to people, objects, possessions, situations, and above all to our own body and life, and when they change, or cease to be, we experience suffering. Nurtured by the desire for permanence and non-change, "one's mind becomes stiff and frozen."[14]

Our greatest enemy is our selfishness, or as Buddhists say, ego-grasping, our self-cherishing attitude. All sufferings derive from it. The three poisons of the mind—greed, hatred, and igno-rance—pollute our thoughts and actions and bring us confusion, restlessness, and pain. And as we scrutinize our own experiences, we find out that with our actions, conscious or unconscious, whether motivated by positive or negative thoughts, we plant seeds that will ripen in the future. Buddhists would say we will suffer, or benefit, from the consequences in future lives, but also, and very much so, in this life, indeed in our immediate future. This is the simple and inexorable law of cause and effect, or karma. The actions that inevitably produce future, if not imme-diate suffering and harm to ourselves or others are called non-virtuous, unskillful, or negative actions, while those that produce positive results are called virtuous actions.

As Buddhists repeatedly tell us, all beings, without exception, share in common the desire to avoid suffering and achieve hap-piness. Yet through our thoughts and actions, and due to our deluded and polluted mind, we bring to ourselves the exact oppo-site of what we strive for.

For Buddhists, sins are called "nonvirtuous actions." By "virtue" they mean not only goodness and morality, but also effi-cacy, power, which virtuous actions indeed are capable of gener-ating. Greed, pride, anger, and the like, then, are nonvirtuous actions that lead to mental suffering and confusion.[15]

As human beings we have the precious opportunity and infi-nite possibilities to activate higher tendencies and plant virtuous seeds that lead to spiritual growth, and ultimately liberation. It all depends on our mind. When we have "hit the bottom" and have become disgusted with our misery, our endless samsaric tur-moil, we develop a renounced mind.

> The gateway to all spiritual paths, whether leading to per-sonal Liberation or Supreme Enlightenment, is the Fully Renounced Mind. Just as a passport, visa, vaccinations and sufficient money are necessary before we can under-take a long journey, so also is this state of mind essential

if we are to follow the Dharma successfully.... What exactly does such a mind renounce? We must develop renunciation of the causes of suffering, the mental afflictions themselves.... Renunciation does not imply that we should give up our enjoyments or possessions. There have been many highly realized beings who have been kings, wealthy merchants and the like. It is not our possessions but our ignorant, clinging attitude towards them that must be abandoned.[16]

It needs to be emphasized that, contrary to popular belief, what the mind renounces is suffering, samsara, a miserable alienated way of life, the existential despair—or to put it differently, it renounces unconsciousness, darkness of the mind, the mind that is not awakened. When the mind is conscious, awakened, then samsara is no more, there is no dissatisfaction. Indeed the word *buddha* means simply that—awakened one.

The mind has the potential to be awakened; in fact it has an urge to awake, yet it sleeps in ignorance and delusions. When unobstructed by ignorance it experiences peace and bliss. Some, if not most people, have such experiences at least a few rare times in their lives: genuine love, aesthetic experiences, encounters with extraordinary human beings, altered states of consciousness. These are brief, fleeting moments when we have a glimpse of another state of mind, another level of existence, and a recognition that it is within our power to attain it, here and now. We also come to realize that it is not the external environment, but our mind, our own inner world, that adjudicates over our happiness or suffering. This is like finding a wish-fulfilling jewel.

But the fully renounced mind in itself is not sufficient to achieve full enlightenment, according to the Mahayana school, which consistently stresses that any action must be motivated by the intention to benefit others and not merely oneself. Thus to the concept of the renounced mind must be added "the mind of enlightenment," the enlightened motive, or so-called *bodhichitta,* which constitutes the second of the three principal aspects of the path to enlightenment.

With the awakening of the mind of enlightenment, one becomes vitally interested in the welfare of other beings. In fact, Tibetan Buddhists always refer to all sentient beings, not only humankind. "Like oneself, all sentient beings are afflicted by suffering; thus even the smallest insect is similar to oneself in not wanting suffering and wanting happiness."[17] From the awareness of the interior states of mind, conscious and unconscious, and the law of cause and effect that determines them, one reaches an expanded awareness that includes others. From ego-involvement, a self-cherishing attitude focusing solely on one's own being, one moves on to another level where one perceives the advantages and necessity to cherish others.

Here too the law of cause and effect reigns supreme. From close interpersonal relationships, to social and international relations, the roots of all conflicts and wars lie in self-cherishing attitudes. Virtuous actions toward others—in body, speech, and mind—such as refraining from killing, stealing, lying, using harsh language, and developing compassion and generosity, bring genuine and lasting pleasure and satisfaction. These actions, free from egocentricity, have an energizing effect on the person who performs them, and paradoxically by losing one's ego in a selfless activity one finds one's Self.

The effects can be easily checked: these are the best moments in anyone's life. They are found in the presence of works of art of any kind—which is precisely the function of art—in true communication with another human being, in creative activity. They are found, though, even in small, simple acts of everyday life, whenever one steps out of one's self-imposed egocentric prison.[18] The enlightened motive moves one, first to be concerned with the sufferings of others, and as a next step to develop a strong motivation to attain enlightenment for the sake of others, that is, to guide them to liberation. This is the way of the bodhisattva who knows that the only way to inspire, assist, and guide others to liberation is to have first followed the path oneself and attained enlightenment. But even before one has made that determination, every action that has been touched by the mind of enlightenment, bodhichitta, even the smallest, most mundane action, becomes powerful. Thus, "it is said that giving a handful of food to a dog if done with bodhicitta, brings us more benefit than giving a universe of jewels to every living being without such motivation."[19]

The third of the three principal aspects of the path to enlightenment is the correct view of reality, or the wisdom of voidness, *shunyata.* This is the most difficult concept to comprehend, and it must be grasped through direct experience not merely through intellectual understanding. Yet it is at the heart of all Buddhist teachings and inseparable from the two other principal aspects of the path. It cannot be explained and understood through rational analysis but only through gradual development of intuitive wisdom. The training in this higher wisdom is essential because misconceptions about reality are the basic source of all suffering.

> The ego's misconceptions about reality...keeps us in bondage, whether it be the iron bondage of worldly existence or the golden bondage of a spiritual way of life. The iron bondage is our continual mental and physical suffering in the cycle of dissatisfied existence known as samsara, while the golden bondage is that of being enslaved to misconceptions and false philosophies.... The highest goal is to be free of *all* bondage.[20]

The concept of shunyata, emptiness, has given rise to much misinterpretation and distortion. *Shunya,* a Sanskrit word, means "relating to the swollen." According to the Buddhist scholar Edward Conze, the etymology of the word expresses the unity of opposites, namely what is swollen from the outside is hollow inside; our personality is both swollen by the five *skandhas*[21] and empty of a self.[22] There is no independent, inherently existent, unrelated self, or "I" as we have been accustomed to think. The nature of all phenomena is emptiness. Philosophically, this is the principle of relativity of all things and conditions. But it is also the principle of limitless potentiality, non-exclusiveness: emptiness can contain and produce everything. A synonym for shunyata is non-duality. On this subject the *Lankavatara Sutra* says:

> ...what is meant by non-duality? It means that light and shade, long and short, black and white, are relative terms...and not independent of each other; as Nirvana and Samsara are, all things are not-two. There is no Nirvana except where is Samsara; there is no Samsara except where is Nirvana; for the condition of existence is not of mutually exclusive character.[23]

The lack of a separate, permanent "I" does not imply its total nonexistence, which would be nihilism, another extreme and dogmatic viewpoint, equally wrong. Thus there is a conventional "I" that we all have, that exists on the relative level of reality, while on the ultimate, absolute level of reality it does not exist. The existence of the five skandhas is conventional truth, while the void nature of all phenomena is absolute truth.[24] This distinction between the relative, mundane, and absolute, ultimate truth is central to the philosophy of Madhyamaka (Middle Way), (which I shall return to in a later chapter). According to the present Dalai Lama, it is "a theory which remains supreme among all the theories of different Buddhist schools."[25] At this point it is important to emphasize again the Buddhist view that the misconception about reality and the belief in an independent, fixed existence of the self is the source of all suffering, and that "realization of sunyata is like the knife that cuts the root of ignorance."[26]

TANTRIC BUDDHISM — VAJRAYANA

With tantric Buddhism or Vajrayana—the third vehicle, although part of the Mahayana school—Tibetan Buddhism reaches its highest and most magnificent development. By following the short path of tantra—also known as the Diamond Vehicle—the adept may reach enlightenment in one single lifetime, while according to Buddhist thought all other graded paths take an extraordinarily long time, "aeon upon aeon," to attain buddhahood.

Tantra, a Sanskrit word, relates to the concept of weaving, suggesting activity, continuity, and also interdependence and interrelatedness. Tantric Buddhism is based on the philosophy of Madhyamaka, which is essentially the concept of the middle way, the view free of the two extremes: eternalism and nihilism. It is interested neither in theoretical and metaphysical speculations, nor in the ascetic practices of some other sects. Its emphasis is on the method, on activity and continuity. The methods are complex, at times bewildering, strange, and incomprehensible to the uninitiated, suggestive of primitive superstition and shamanic magic. Yet in their essence they are all but different methods of spiritual transformation: ways of transmuting any and all aspects of samsaric life—positive, negative, or neutral—into transcendental wisdom. All obstacles, negativities, passions are harnessed and transmuted into vehicles on the path to enlightenment. Good and evil are transcended and flow back into pure spiritual essence, which is the ultimate nature of the universe. This is the direct, short path to liberation, the most powerful one, as it entails a radical revolution of consciousness, but it is by no means an easy path, nor devoid of dangers. It is far from being primitive (in the negative sense of that term); quite to the contrary, it is a most sophisticated method of spiritual growth and transformation. Mircea Eliade points out that there are parallels between

> ...tantrism and the great Western mystero-sophic current that, at the beginning of the Christian era, arose from the

confluence of Gnosticism, Hermetism, Greco-Egyptian alchemy, and the traditions of the Mysteries.[27]

The goal is the same as in all other schools of Buddhism—namely, enlightenment—but it is enlightenment here and now, and not in any inconceivable future. It aims at the permanent destruction of suffering—the sole concern of Buddha as expressed in his very first sermon on the four noble truths—and follows the conviction that there is an alternative in this existence to the misery of mundane life. It is important to note that before entering the tantric path the adept must be familiar with and practice at all times the fundamental steps of the Hinayana and Mahayana schools. Restraint, self-awareness, training of the mind, compassion, and cultivation of wisdom are necessary foundations before one ventures into the diamond path. In fact a tantric master of the eleventh century, Atisha, "based his teaching on the idea that Hinayana, Mahayana and Vajrayana could not be regarded separately but must be seen as aspects of a single path."[28] Looking at the three yanas together, they are a consistent and natural evolution in Buddhist theory and practice.

Tantra implies continuity—the continuity of the movement of one's life and inner growth, when spiritual practice is consciously pursued. And practice leads to an understanding of the interwovenness of all phenomena, the relationship between microcosm and macrocosm, mind and universe, matter and spirit—an idea that bears a striking similarity to the findings of modern science.

It could be said that the aim of Buddhist tantra is to penetrate into, harness, and transform the dynamic forces of the universe, which are no different from the psychological forces and archetypal constellations of our own psyche. But this cannot be done through the exercise of discursive thought or application of abstract theories, but only by being deeply immersed in actual practices. Due to the enormous wealth of those practices,[29] tantra has given rise to many misunderstandings and misconceptions. In the Western world it has often been equated with magic and exotic sexual practices.

As to the origins of the tantra, as well as the similarity or differences between Hindu and Buddhist tantras, there is much controversy and no definitive agreement. According to one author, there was no one particular person who introduced tantra into Buddhism at any particular time, but rather that it has been gradually incorporated in the course of centuries.[30] The same author maintains that there are no fundamental differences between Hindu and Buddhist tantras.[31]

Other scholars, by contrast, such as Lama Govinda and Benoytosh Bhattacharyya maintain that tantric Buddhism is not an offspring of tantric Hinduism, as claimed by some; it was crystallized into a definitive form by the third century A.D. Both scholars affirm that despite outward appearances of similarity between the two systems, there are fundamental differences. The main difference, according to Lama Govinda, lies in the concept of *shakti,* the active power, and the creative feminine aspect of *Shiva,* the highest god. This aspect does not enter into the system of tantric Buddhism. In the latter the central idea is not *shakti*—power, but *prajna*—knowledge, intuitive wisdom.[32] It would be hard though to differentiate wisdom and power in the context of Vajrayana. Wisdom ultimately is power, albeit not the power of the sword, but the force capable of affecting transformation, and Buddhists repeatedly talk about the power of the mind.

These issues may not be of major significance as far as the practice of Vajrayana is concerned. However, since there is considerable confusion on this point, it is important to be aware of them, and to recognize the proper distinctions as well as the equivalents between the two tantric systems.

The polarity of male and female principles is a basic Vajrayana concept, and their union is the goal of all tantric practices. Through this union of opposites all duality is transcended into an absolute unity. This is the highest spiritual reality in the path to enlightenment—in fact it is enlightenment itself.

In Buddhist iconography the principle of union is represented by deities and their consorts in ecstatic embrace, enjoying great bliss.

> According to all schools of Tantra, bliss is the nature of the Absolute.... The Absolute is realized by us when we realize our self as perfect bliss. In all our ordinary experiences of pleasure we have but a momentary glimpse of the same bliss as constitutes the ultimate nature of our self. But these experiences of pleasure, because of their extremely limited and defiled nature, bind us to a lower plane of life, instead of contributing to our advancement towards self-realisation.[33]

Bliss, nirvana, enlightenment become synonymous in tantric Buddhism—the total immersion of the ultimate nature of the self and the not-self in the oneness of the perfect bliss.[34] The sexoyogic spiritual practices—the erotic mysticism, so much misunderstood in the West—are based on that principle, when sexual bliss becomes divine bliss and the instrument for highest spiritual attainment.

Buddhist tantra holds that the human body is the microcosm that embodies the truth of the macrocosm. Absolute reality contains all dualities and polarities: noumenon and phenomenon, potentiality and manifestation, nirvana and samsara, *prajna* (wisdom—female principle) and *upaya* (method to attain wisdom—male principle), *shunya* (void) and *karuna* (compassion). Within their own bodies tantric disciples achieve the reunion of the two polar principles, that is, the primordial unity that excludes all discrimination and includes all differentiations. Or, in other words, through the medium of their bodies they transcend the mundane, phenomenal world and experience nonduality, the completeness preceding all creation, the great bliss. All tantric practices, rituals, and meditations—the so-called *sadhanas*—have as their aim this realization.

This is the dialectic of opposites, the theme of the Madhyamaka philosophy, the Middle Way, that encompasses and embraces all. But tantric disciples are more concerned with direct knowledge of that state, achieved in the actuality of their practice.

> Right in that moment when the Great Compassion arises
> Emerges nakedly and vividly the Great Voidness.
> Let me always find this unmistakable Two-in-One Path
> And practice it day and night.[35]

The Tibetan Buddhist symbol of the two-in-one is *yab-yum,* the father-mother divine couple in embrace, seen in Tibetan sacred art, and which both inspires and expresses visually the experiences and visions of meditation. Lama Govinda states that in these symbols there is no association whatever with physical sexuality. They portray only the union of male and female principles—the eternal female qualities, as those of the "Divine Mother," or transcendental wisdom. "...Instead of seeking union with a woman outside ourselves, we have to seek it *within ourselves*...by the union of our male and female nature in the process of meditation."[36] Lama Govinda holds the view that sexual polarity has to be recognized as a mere incident of universal polarity and has to be overcome.[37]

> Only if we are able to see the relationship of body and mind, of physical and spiritual interaction in a universal perspective, and if in this way we overcome the "I" and "mine" and the whole structure of egocentric feelings, opinions, and prejudices, which produce the illusion of our separate individuality, then only can we rise into the sphere of Buddhahood.[38]

Nevertheless conjugal intercourse *(maithuna)* has been practiced by tantric Buddhists as a sacred ritual, based on the same concept of the union of male and female principles. S. B. Dasgupta examines the argument of the tantric Buddhists in defense of their unconventional practice of *maithuna*. They emphasize that everything depends on the purity of the mind: actions motivated by and done with wisdom and compassion, with a pure mind, cannot but be pure. But they also warn that it is a very dangerous path for the uninitiated. "That which drags the uninitiated fool to the hell of debauchery may help the initiated yogin to attain enlightenment."[39] The vital point is the adherence of the yogi and yogini to their vow to perform any action with a compassionate mind and with wisdom, that is, the knowledge and understanding of the void nature of all phenomena. So it is said that:

> As some medicine is sweet to taste and at the same time cures disease, so also is the bliss coming out of the combination of Prajna (wisdom) and Upaya (compassion)— it destroys the afflictions easily and smoothly.... Again, what to one is a rope for hanging oneself, is the remover of bondage to the other."[40]

Another scholar, Herbert Guenther, similarly argues in favor of pleasure as being a life-enhancing state. "We may use such phrases as 'ecstatic bliss' or 'great bliss' to refer to the sense of freedom from the impoverishment brought about by ego-centredness."[41] Here is how some of the tantric texts speak on the subject of bliss:

> The All-Buddha-Awareness which is experienced within ourselves
> Is called Great Bliss because it is the most excellent pleasure of all pleasures.
> Without bliss there is no enlightenment, for enlightenment is bliss itself.
> Just as in deep darkness the moon-stone spreads its light,
> So this supreme Great Bliss in a moment dissipates all misery.[42]

This is by no means hedonism; quite to the contrary it requires extraordinary discipline, and it is only through consistent discipline that true freedom is acquired. On the path toward freedom any passion and desire must be utilized and transformed into wisdom. This is the very basic principle of any tantric practice. In this respect it is similar to homeopathy, working on the principle that like cures like. The very same element that causes a disease may if applied in a proper dose act as an antidote and a cure.

> The Vajrayanist will also say that the very action which binds a man down to the world of infinite misery may help him to attain liberation, if taken from a different perspective, i.e., if taken with the knowledge of the Prajna and the Upaya.[43]

As in homeopathic medicine, symptoms are not suppressed but rather caused to exacerbate temporarily as a necessary step toward their complete elimination. Thus anger is cured with anger, desire with desire, and so on when transmuted into wisdom.

But we are dealing here with a double-edged sword: the way may lead to illumination or pathology. For this reason the path cannot be followed without the guidance of a qualified compassionate teacher who himself has attained wisdom. This is also the reason why the teachings and actual practices have been kept secret: to achieve the desired effect and value, they can be transmitted only through a highly developed teacher, and under proper circumstances. But in fact they are bound to remain secret to the uninitiated for, like any esoteric teachings, they can be communicated only gradually and to the extent that one is ready to receive them, or rather to discover them for oneself.

In the process of transformation and the achievement of higher states of consciousness, numerous aids are used and a great variety of worships and rituals practiced. They are all designed to involve totally the three aspects of our being, that is, body, speech, and mind. Their purpose is to activate and conjure up powerful but dormant forces from the deep levels of the unconscious; it is a confrontation with our innermost nature to awaken us.

The three basic and prevalent methods are: recitation of mantras (sacred words) involving the speech; performance of ritual gestures (mudras) involving the body; meditation (especially visualization of and identification with deities) involving the mind.

I shall return to these methods in a subsequent chapter and discuss them and their meaning in more detail, as well as the symbolism and function of mandalas. At this point it may suffice to state that:

> The aim of all the tantras is to teach the ways whereby we may set free the divine light which is mysteriously present and shining in each one of us, although it is enveloped in an insidious web of the psyche's weaving.[44]

2 Carl Gustav Jung

Two and a half millennia after Buddha and about a century ago, on the other side of the globe from India, Carl Gustav Jung was born. He was born and lived his entire life in Switzerland, in that lovely, peaceful country in the heart of Europe and the Western world, the country that has known no wars for many, many years. His parents and ancestors on both sides were traditional people, deeply rooted in the Swiss soil and customs, which endure and tolerate no change. He loved his country, but from an early age he felt that its beauty belonged to a space and a time that far transcended the narrow boundaries of that tiny nation and its immovable society. His very first memories—first intimation of something larger than himself—were memories of wonder as he stood in awesome contemplation of the blue waters of Lake Constance, and the white, snow-covered peaks of the majestic Alps. Already then he had a sense that this was the center of the universe—not the universe of his parents and the few million Swiss, but of a very private universe within himself that he saw mirrored in the quiet waters of the lake, and extending to the peaks of the Alps, and beyond into infinity.

He grew up as a shy, sensitive boy, often at odds with his parents' beliefs and his teachers' demands. He felt both very special and at times inadequate in school in comparison to his classmates. He was easily hurt and was prone to outbursts of rage when injustice was done to him—when, for example, his teacher accused him of cheating. But it was in such moments that he sought and found refuge in his personality Number Two, as he used to call it. This personality was his true authentic self, reaching deep into the roots of mankind itself, perhaps even before mankind was.

> Somewhere deep in the background I always knew that I was two persons. One was the son of my parents, who went to school and was less intelligent, attentive, hardworking, decent, and clean than many other boys. The other was grown up—old, in fact—skeptical, mistrustful, remote from the world of men, but close to nature, the earth, the sun, the moon, the weather, all living creatures, and above all close to the night, to dreams, and to whatever "God" worked directly in him.[45]

This "other" was a fragile, frail personality that often eluded him, and so he had to push forward with his so-called personality Number One, a sham, a game, one that gradually more and more satisfied all around him, but not his own self. So he continued his path, going from one success to another; whatever he worked at he accomplished with flying colors. But the turmoil inside never left him and was a constant prodder that led him astray from where everyone around him expected him to go: while his personality Number One was brilliant, his personality Number Two was aching with pain, the pain of unfulfilled wholeness. He searched for that wholeness all his life.

He heard of a professor in Vienna. He went to see the professor and paid his respect to him, as he mistook the professor for a genius who was not understood by others. They became close friends and associates. Jung's personality Number Two, however, rebelled at the very instance of their first encounter. But he refused to heed his personality Number Two, which was still weak and submerged at that time. The professor in Vienna became famous, and as his fame grew their friendship dwindled. Only later Jung understood: it was not their friendship that dwindled, it was his personality Number Two that became an individual in his own right. The professor from Vienna and Jung parted. This was the greatest shock in his life. It threw him into darkness such as he had never known before. But out of it his entire work emerged.

He had left behind not only his friend from Vienna, to whom he nevertheless always remained grateful, but also his personality Number One. From then on Jung devoted himself fully to his personality Number Two. Many people from all the corners of the world came to see him and inspire him, as he inspired them. Alone in his stone tower he was in deep and intimate contact with everything and everyone that was at that time, that preceded him, and would follow him. On a stormy day in late spring, at the age of eighty-five, his long and rich life came to an end. His personality Number One finally left him for good. But his personality Number Two goes on living, for there was no time when it was not and there can be no time it will cease to be.

"My life has been in a sense the quintessence of what I have written,"[46] says C. G. Jung in the introduction to his autobiography. So his entire life, his myth, should be viewed as an indivisible whole that proceeded as a gradual and continuous unfoldment out of its own unique seed. No event, no aspect of his outer or inner life, is unimportant or irrelevant to his work.

> My life is what I have done, my scientific work; the one is inseparable from the other. The work is the expression of my inner development; for commitment to the contents of the unconscious forms the man and produces his transformations. My works can be regarded as stations along my life's way.[47]

There was a particularly pregnant time in Jung's life, a time when new ideas were germinating that were to occupy him for the rest of his life. This was the period following his break with Freud, when for a while he lost his bearings. It was a time of confusion, turmoil, isolation, loneliness—of inner chaos. Jung was assailed with confusing dreams, images, visions, a surge of unconscious material that at times made him doubt his own sanity. And indeed, in a sense it was not unlike a psychotic break. But it was also a crucial intersection, a most creative station along his life's way. These were the years of Jung's confrontation with his unconscious.

Here the vision of the young Siddhartha Gautama comes back to our mind. The well-protected innocent prince suddenly shocked by the sights of the tragic side of life—sickness, old age, and death—his determination to find answers to the riddle of life, first unsuccessfully from learned men, and finally from within himself, in deep meditation under the bodhi tree. Similarly, Jung could not find answers to his questions either from Freud or anyone else, from any books and theories, and so like Siddhartha, he left behind all of them to look for answers within his own psyche. In his autobiography Jung tells us he had to undergo the original experience himself. One day he sat at his desk, let himself drop, and plunged into the depths of his psyche, submitting to the spontaneous impulses of his unconscious.[48] This was the very beginning of an experiment that lasted for several years and produced a wealth of material, later to become part of Jung's most important works, his most creative contributions. Throughout that time he not only observed carefully but wrote down, and embellished with drawings, his dreams, fantasies, and visions, and they all became part of his famous Red Book. But being trained as a scientist, he felt the obligation to understand the meaning of all that material. "I had to draw concrete conclusions from the insight the unconscious had given me—and that task was to become a life's work."[49] He had to show that his very personal, subjective experiences were potential experiences of all humankind, for they were an inherent part of the nature of the psyche.[50] It was, though, a revolutionary way in scientific methodology, "a new way of seeing things."[51] Above all Jung had to prove that his own experiences were real, which others could have too: that the unconscious was a demonstrable psychic reality, but which had its own style and spoke its own language, namely the universal language of images and symbols. Furthermore Jung became aware that the insights gained from the unconscious must be translated into an ethical obligation.

> Not to do so is to fall prey to the power principle, and this produces dangerous effects which are destructive not only to others but even to the knower. The images of the unconscious place a great responsibility upon a man. Failure to understand them, or a *shirking of ethical responsibility, deprives him of his wholeness and imposes a painful fragmentariness on his life.*[52]

This thought is reminiscent of Buddhist ethics, as enunciated in the eightfold path, particularly in right action and right meditation. Personal suffering cannot be eliminated, and individual wholeness achieved, when ethical conduct is not observed. Jung understood, as Buddha pointed out long ago, that mere ego-centered pursuits in disregard of others lead to confusion. Thus knowledge acquired through contact with the unconscious—through "right meditation"—in order to have any significance, must become an integral part of one's life; it must be translated into "right action."

After about six years of a fierce struggle with the darkness of his unconscious, Jung began to have the first inklings of light. The dawn appeared when he started sketching mandalas—one new mandala every day. A *mandala*, the Sanskrit word for circle, is the circular pattern form found in all elements of nature, and in the arts and dances of all people, throughout history. It is also an image residing in the depths of the human psyche that spontaneously emerges and assumes many different forms. It usually takes shape in times of disorganization and inner chaos, and it is nature's way of restoring balance and order. Jung discovered, through his own experience, that each single mandala he drew was an expression of his inner state of being at that particular time. As his psychic state changed so did the mandala he would spontaneously sketch. He came to the conclusion that the mandala represented "Formation, Transformation, Eternal Mind's eternal recreation."[53] At the same time he realized that the efforts he pursued consciously, prompted so to speak by his personality Number One, were undermined by a stronger force that compelled him to take a different path. In other words, he could not choose a goal, rather it chose him.

> I had to let myself be carried along by the current, without a notion of where it would lead me. When I began drawing the mandalas, however, I saw that everything, all the paths I had been following, all the steps I had taken, were leading back to a single point—namely, to the mid-point. It became increasingly plain to me that the mandala is the center. It is the exponent of all paths. It is the path to the center, to individuation.[54]

Thus the forceful and persistent question in his mind was answered—the question as to what this process is all about and what its destination is. The goal was the Self, the alpha and omega of psychic development, for the Self is the *proto-image* out of which the person emerges, and the culmination of his growth.

And then Jung had a dream that was symbolic of his situation at the time (darkness and isolation, but also an emerging vision of light and flowering of new life), and through its elaborate imagery unmistakably pointed to the center, the Self, as the goal.

> Through this dream I understood that the Self is the principle and archetype of orientation and meaning. Therein lies its healing function. For me, this insight signified an approach to the center and therefore to the goal. Out of this emerged a first inkling of my personal myth.[55]

This was an event of tremendous importance, a turning point in Jung's life and his work. It was the climax of his confrontation with the unconscious, his six years of solitary battle with the dark depths of his psyche. Jung describes these years as

> the most important in my life—in them everything essential was decided. It all began then; the later details are only supplements and clarifications of the material that burst forth from the unconscious, and at first swamped me. It was the *prima materia* for a lifetime's work.[56]

It was during those years that he made the discovery of the collective unconscious and developed the concepts of the archetypes and the Self. But much work still lay ahead of him: all the fantasies and material that had flooded him from the unconscious and the insights he gained needed to be built on a solid foundation of scientific theory. That work gradually unfolded as Jung encountered alchemy.

In alchemy he discovered that, unlike in Christianity, the feminine principle is as important as the masculine. The symbols in alchemy, "those old acquaintances" of Jung, fascinated him.[57] But he began really to understand it after reading a Chinese alchemical text, *The Secret of the Golden Flower*.[58] This was also probably the beginning of his interest in Oriental philosophies and spiritual traditions. To Jung "the secret of the alchemy was in…the transformation of personality through the blending and fusion of the noble with the base components…of the conscious with the unconscious."[59] In alchemy he found a correspondence to his psychology, which gave his work a confirmation of its validity. It was not, however, the end product of Jung's creative journey, for he did not stop with psychology: he went beyond it.

COLLECTIVE UNCONSCIOUS

Jung's greatest contribution to psychology was his theory of the collective unconscious. He argued that this concept was not a speculative idea or a philosophical postulate, but that there was an empirical proof for it.[60] He defines the collective unconscious as the part of the psyche that owes its existence exclusively to heredity, and not to personal experiences that had been conscious at one time and then disappeared from consciousness. The latter is the layer of the psyche that he calls the personal unconscious and that contains all the material that the individual has merely forgotten or repressed, either deliberately or unintentionally.[61] Thus Jung makes the distinction between the personal unconscious, the subjective psyche, and the objective psyche that he calls the impersonal, transpersonal, or collective unconscious. He discovered the collective unconscious through his own dreams and visions, as well as those of his patients, including fantasies of schizophrenics. He observed that all this material often contained mythological motifs and religious symbols. Jung then came to the following conclusion:

> In addition to our immediate consciousness, which is of a thoroughly personal nature and which we believe to be the only empirical psyche (even if we tack on the personal unconscious as an appendix), there exists a second psychic system of a collective, universal, and impersonal nature which is identical in all individuals. This collective unconscious does not develop individually but is inherited. It consists of pre-existent forms, the archetypes, which can only become conscious secondarily and which give definite form to certain psychic contents.[62]

ARCHETYPES

According to Jung, archetypes—the contents of the collective unconscious—are analogous to instincts. Both are fundamental dynamic forces in the human personality that pursue their inherent goals, in the psychic or physiological organisms respectively.

Jung also refers to archetypes as primordial images, "the most ancient and the most universal thought-form of humanity. They are as much feelings as thoughts."[63] But it should be stressed that archetypes are not inherited ideas; they are merely propensities in the human psyche that can express themselves in specific forms and meaning when activated.

> There are as many archetypes as there are typical situations in life. Endless repetition has engraved these experiences into our psychic constitution, not in the form of images filled with content, but at first only as *forms without content,* representing merely the possibility of a certain type of perception and action. When a situation occurs which corresponds to a given archetype, that archetype becomes activated and a compulsiveness appears, which, like an instinctual drive, gains its way against all reason and Will....[64]

In developing the concept of archetypes and their dynamism, Jung quotes a remarkable example: the genesis of the idea of conservation of energy, credited to Robert Mayer in the nineteenth century. The latter was not a physicist who might be naturally preoccupied with such a concept, but a physician, and the idea came to him in a most extraordinary way, during a voyage in the tropics. Here is what Mayer wrote about his experience and discovery:

> I'm far from having hatched out the theory at my writing desk. [He then reports certain physiological observations he had made...as ship's doctor.] Now, if one wants to be clear on matters of physiology, some knowledge of physical processes is essential, unless one prefers to work at things from the metaphysical side, which I find infinitely disgusting. I therefore held fast to physics and stuck to the subject with such fondness that, although many may

laugh at me for this, I paid but little attention to that remote quarter of the globe in which we were, preferring to remain on board where I could work without intermission, and where I passed many an hour as though *inspired*, the like of which I cannot remember either before or since. Some flashes of thought that passed through me while in the roads of Surabaya were at once assiduously followed up, and in their turn led to fresh subjects. Those lines have passed, but the quiet examination of that which then came to the surface in me has taught me that it is a truth, which cannot only be subjectively felt, but objectively proved. It remains to be seen whether this can be accomplished by a man so little versed in physics as I am.[65]

The question that Jung asked himself is: where did this new idea come from and impose itself upon consciousness, and what is the force behind it that overwhelmed the personality? And the answer can be found only in applying his theory of archetypes, that is, that "the idea of energy and its conservation must be a primordial image that was dormant in the collective unconscious."[66] Jung then proceeds to demonstrate that such a primordial image indeed existed since most primitive times, expressed in many different forms, as for example the idea of demonism, magic power, the soul's immortality, and many others. The notion of energy, its preservation or rather transmutation, is the central concept in all tantras.

THE SELF

As already stated, there are countless archetypes, but the one that encompasses all others, the quintessential archetype, is the Self. It is the organizing, guiding, and uniting principle that gives the personality direction and meaning in life. It is the beginning, the source of the personality and its ultimate goal, the culmination of one's growth, that is, self-realization. The Self is the *homo totus,* the timeless man, that not only expresses his unique individuality and wholeness but is the symbol of man's divinity when he touches the cosmos, his microcosm reflecting the macrocosm.

> Intellectually the Self is no more than a psychological concept, a construct that serves to express an unknowable essence which we cannot grasp as such, since by definition it transcends our powers of comprehension. It might equally well be called the "God within us." The beginnings of our whole psychic life seem to be inextricably rooted in this point, and all our highest and ultimate purposes seem to be striving towards it.[67]

Jung also refers to the Self as being both unitemporal and unique, and universal and eternal, the one expressing man's essence, and the other being a God-image, an archetypal symbol.[68]

INDIVIDUATION

Between the stages of the self as a source in the beginning and the Self as a goal, in its ultimate destination, there is an ongoing continuity of development, which Jung has called the process of individuation. It is the process of integration of the personality. This archetypal, universal psychic process is autonomous and unconscious, and it has run its course since immemorial time. It reflects psyche's striving to harmonize its conscious and unconscious contents, and it is the natural and spontaneous urge for self-realization and wholeness, the quest for meaning. Collectively it has been expressed in the multitudes of myths and symbols in which mankind has given outward form to its inner experiences. On an individual level, although the process always goes on since the psyche never rests, it may remain purely unconscious or it may become a conscious task. Whether it will lead in one direction or the other depends on the intervention of consciousness.

The difference between the two roads is tremendous, and their outcome far reaching. In one instance when consciousness is not involved, "the end remains as dark as the beginning." In the other instance "the personality is permeated with light," and consciousness is further extended and enhanced.[69]

Through alchemy and its symbolism Jung became aware that the transformation of personality takes place in the interaction between the ego and the unconscious, out of which a new unified being emerges. It is a new being, yet not entirely new, for it was always there, but dormant and hidden in the chaos of the unconscious. The process requires an open communication between the conscious mind and its unconscious counterpart, a sensitivity to the signals of the unconscious, which speaks in the language of symbols. It is the constant dialogue between the outer and the inner, the mundane life and its symbolic dimensions—dreams, fantasies, visions.

The arduous task of conscious confrontation with the unconscious has the effect of expanding consciousness, of diminishing the sovereign powers of the unconscious and bringing about the renewal and transformation of personality. This change, which is the central object of alchemy and of Jung's psychotherapy, comes about through the principle that Jung called the transcendent function.[70]

Indeed it is more than an arduous and often painful task, as Jung experienced himself. It is a battle between two opposing forces, each contending for its own rights, the battle between reason and rationality versus chaos and irrationality. At the same time it has to be a collaboration between the conscious and unconscious attitudes of the psyche: consciousness must heed its unconscious counterpart, must listen to the inner voices, so that the latter can cooperate with consciousness instead of disturbing it.

> The confrontation of the two positions generates a tension charged with energy and creates a living, third thing—not a logical stillbirth...but a movement out of

the suspension between opposites, a living birth that leads
to a new level of being....[71]

Since the process aims at the total transformation of personality, nothing that belongs to it, no aspect of it, must be
excluded.[72] And the consummation of this union of opposites, in
order to create new life—not a logical stillbirth—must be
attended not only by Logos, the rational principle, but by Eros
too, the principle of relatedness.[73]

So, individuation leads from oneness, emptiness, the undif-
ferentiated state of unconsciousness, *participation mystique,*[74] to
ever-increasing differentiation, the supremacy of the ego, to oneness, emptiness again, which has become fullness—to the Self,
the mandala. The end has rejoined its beginning, and the ultimate goal its original source.

ALCHEMY

The evolution of personality, or, as Jung called it, the individuation process, has been expressed in different terms by the symbolism of alchemy. Even though the alchemists set themselves the
task of revealing the secrets of matter and chemical transformation, their labor primarily reflected a parallel psychic process,
which met with a strong resonance in Jung's mind and had an
enormous impact on his work.

To Jung the chemical experiments of the alchemists, the
whole alchemical *opus,* was of a psychic nature rather than a
search for the secret of gold-making. The alchemists themselves
proclaimed that *"Aurum nostrum non est aurum vulgi."*[75] While
working in his laboratory the alchemist had certain psychic experiences that he attributed to the properties of the matter; Jung
believed that in fact he was experiencing his own unconscious.
"In seeking to explore it [the matter] he projected the unconscious into the darkness of matter in order to illuminate it."[76]

It has been generally understood that the purpose of alchemy was to produce a miraculous substance, gold, panacea, elixir of life. But in actuality, above and beyond that, the very essence of all alchemical work was a spiritual exercise whose goal was none other than spiritual transformation, liberation of God from the darkness of matter.[77] The bewildering profusion of complicated and often grotesque alchemical symbolism describes pictorially the process of change from psychic sleep to awakening, and the stages along that journey. Jung found in this symbolism an illustration of what he had called the process of individuation: one's gradual unfoldment from an unconscious to a conscious state, and the healing process underlying it.[78]

In medieval European alchemy, which he discovered by way of Chinese alchemy, Jung found the spiritual roots of a Western tradition that addressed itself to the same issues that preoccupied him all his life. Thus alchemy provided him with a historical foundation as well as validation for his own findings.

As in Jung's psychology, opposites and their union play a major role in alchemical procedure. The union is the motivating force and the goal of the process. But at the beginning of the process the opposites form a dualism, conceived in numerous terms such as: upper and lower, cold and warm, spirit (soul) and body, heaven and earth, bright and dark, active and passive, precious and cheap, good and evil, open and hidden, inner and outer, East and West, god and goddess, masculine and feminine.[79]

The primal opposites are consciousness and unconsciousness, whose symbols are Sol and Luna—sun and moon—the one representing the diurnal and the other the nocturnal side of consciousness, the male and female principles. The corresponding alchemical substances are sulfur and salt. Sulfur, because of its association with the sun, is the masculine principle expressing consciousness. In alchemical texts it is referred to as "the male and universal seed," the "spirit of generative power," the "source of illumination and all knowledge." It has a double nature: in its initial crude form it is burning and corrosive and has an offensive odor, but when transmuted, "cleansed of all impurities, it is the matter of our stone."[80] Salt, because of its association with the moon, is the feminine principle and expresses various aspects of the unconscious. Like its counterpart sulfur, salt contains a double nature: in its unrefined form, coming from the sea, it is bitter and harsh, like tears and sorrow, yet at the same time it is the mother of wisdom when transmuted. As the principle of Eros, it connects everything. Salt is also associated with earth, and as such represents the Great Mother and the archetype of the feminine deity.

Starting with the original substance, the *prima materia* that contains the opposites, the alchemist's task is to harmonize them, to bring them into unity, which culminates in the "chymical marriage," the consummation of his work. Jung postulates that on a psychological level the union of opposites cannot be achieved by the conscious ego alone—by reason, analysis—which separates and divides; nor even by the unconscious alone—which unites; it needs a third element, the transcendent function. In the same way, for the conjunction to take place, the alchemist needed a third factor, a medium, which was Mercurius (mercury). Thus there is sulfur, the masculine principle, salt, its feminine counterpart, and mercury, the substance that is both liquid and solid. By nature Mercurius is androgynous and partakes of both the masculine and feminine elements; in himself he unites the spiritual and physical, the highest and lowest.

Alchemy is full of paradoxes—as Jung's work is—since paradoxes are the only way remotely to express the inexpressible, the phenomena of the psyche that can be apprehended only through direct experience.[81] The mysterious Mercurius is the paradox *par excellence*. The fertile imagination of the alchemists gave countless synonyms to Mercurius, and the most fantastic descriptions of his attributes. Here is one example, taken from an alchemical treatise, in which the alchemist asks nature to tell him about her son Mercurius, and she responds:

Know that I have only one such son; he is one of seven,

and the first among them; and though he is now all
things, he was at first only one. In him are the four elements, yet he is not an element. He is a spirit, yet he has
a body; a man, yet he performs a woman's part; a boy, yet
he bears a man's weapons; a beast, yet he has the wings
of a bird. He is poison, yet he cures leprosy; life, yet he
kills all things; a King, yet another occupies his throne; he
flees from the fire, yet fire is taken from him; he is water,
yet does not wet the hands; he is earth, yet is sown; he is
air and lives by water.[82]

Jung recognized in the multiple and paradoxical aspects of
Mercurius a reflection of the nature of the self, which is a *com-
plexio oppositorum,* and must necessarily be such if it is to sym-
bolize man's totality. To Jung, Mercurius represented not only
the self but the individuation process as well, and because of the
limitless number of his names, also the collective unconscious.[83]

The first phase of the alchemical process was the black stage,
nigredo, characterized by confusion, frustration, depression, "the
dark night of the soul" of St. John of the Cross, in which nevertheless all potentialities and the seeds of future development are
contained. Then as the fire of the alchemical retort, the psychic
fire, purges the elements, the second white phase, *albedo,* is
brought about. It is the stage of clarification and intensification
of life and consciousness. The final phase is the red stage, when
the drama reaches its conclusion: the chemical process of *con-
iunctio,* the appearance of the philosophers' stone, and at the
same time the completion of psychic synthesis—the emergence of
the Self.

What is the philosophers' stone, the lapis? It was said that it
heals and bestows immortality. To Jung "the lapis is a fabulous
entity of cosmic dimensions which surpasses human understanding." Like "man's totality, the Self, [it] is by definition
beyond the bounds of knowledge."[84]

However, to the alchemist Gerhard Dorn, the lapis was not

the completion of the art. The final and highest conjunction was the union of the whole human being with *unus mundus,* the one world. This is when the individual psyche touches eternity, the identity of the personal with the transpersonal. It is the numinous event, the mystery of the *unio mystica,* or in the Oriental traditions, the experiences of *tao, samadhi,* or *satori.*[85]

Jung concluded that the phases of the alchemical procedures, the reconciliation of conflicting opposites into a unity, paralleled the stages of the individuation process.[86] In his dreams, as well as those of his patients, he could at times discern a portrayal of the mandala, symbolizing the multiplicity of the phenomenal world within an underlying unity. The mandala symbolism represents the psychological equivalent of *unus mundus,* while its parapsychological equivalent is Jung's concept of synchronicity.

Synchronicity

All of Jung's discoveries were accompanied by dreams or synchronistic events that either pointed the way or gave him confirmation that he was proceeding in the right direction. At the time when he was diligently drawing mandalas, he produced a painting of a golden castle. The painting was particularly intriguing because of its Chinese quality, and he was puzzled by it. Shortly afterward he received from the sinologist Richard Wilhelm a copy of *The Secret of the Golden Flower,* an old Chinese alchemical text, which marked the beginning of his fascination with alchemy. The event of receiving the Chinese manuscript was a synchronistic one, and furthermore it was connected with a mandala painting of Jung's. This striking coincidence, this single event, contained in itself both the mandala symbolism and the principle of synchronicity, namely, the double expression of *unus mundus*—psychological and parapsychological. And indeed Jung felt the powerful effect one experiences in moments of encounter with the *unus mundus.* This event occurred at the time when the cycle of his alienation was drawing to a close. In his autobiography Jung remembers: "That was the first event which broke my isolation. I became aware of an affinity: I could establish ties with something and someone."[87] Perhaps it is not a mere coincidence that Jung for the first time announced to the world his concept of synchronicity in a memorial address to his friend Richard Wilhelm, the man who played such a significant part at a crucial period in Jung's life.

Synchronicity is the most abstract and most elusive of Jung's concepts. Jung describes synchronicity as "a *meaningful coincidence* of two or more events, where something other than the probability of chance is involved."[88] The connections of events are not the result of the principle of cause and effect, but of something else that Jung called an acausal connecting principle. The critical factor is the meaning, the subjective experience that comes to the person: events are connected in a meaningful way, that is, events of the inner and outer world, the invisible and the tangible, the mind and the physical universe. This coming together at the right moment can happen only without the conscious intervention of the ego. Instead it is prepared in the unconsciousness of the psyche, and it is as though the psyche had its own secret design, irrespective of ego's conscious wishes. Such synchronistic events, of smaller or larger proportions, occur to most people in daily life, but as with dreams, if we do not recognize them and pay attention to them, they remain insignificant.

Jung gives examples from his practice when patients he was treating had uncanny coincidences that put them in touch with a deeper than conscious level of experience, and convinced them in a dramatic, unequivocal way of the reality and limitlessness of the unconscious. Of particular interest is the case of the young, well-educated woman, who, with her very one-sided logical mind, was stubbornly unresponsive to Jung's efforts to soften her rationalism. One day as she was telling her dream of the night before, involving a golden scarab that was given to her, a flying insect persistently knocked at the window obviously attempting to enter the room. Jung opened the window, let the insect in and caught it. The insect turned out to be a golden-green beetle, very much resembling the scarab from the dream.

> I handed the beetle to my patient with the words, "Here is your scarab." This experience punctured the desired hole in her rationalism and broke the ice of her intellectual resistance. The treatment could now be continued with satisfactory results.[89]

In developing his concept of synchronicity, Jung related it to the discoveries of modern theoretical physics, from which we had learned that causality and prediction are no longer valid in the microphysical world.[90] He concluded that there is a common background between microphysics and his depth psychology.[91] At the same time Jung went back to ancient Chinese philosophy and recognized a correspondence between synchronicity and the ineffable idea of tao. In fact it was the *I Ching*, the Chinese *Book of Changes*, and its method, with which Jung had personal experience, that was to him a major inspiration in developing the concept of synchronicity. The two seemingly opposite frameworks, the rational scientific and the intuitive philosophical, are by no means contradictory. In his book, *The Tao of Physics*, Fritjof Capra addresses himself to this very point and argues that there are close parallels between basic concepts of modern physics and Eastern mystical teachings. The findings of theoretical physics reveal a universe that is a harmonious, unified process, a dynamic web of interrelated elements. This is precisely the fundamental thought in Buddhist and Taoist philosophies. And to Jung, synchronistic events point to "a profound harmony between all forms of existence."[92] When experienced as such, the synchronistic event becomes a tremendously powerful occurrence that gives the individual a sense of transcending time and space.

3 Methods in Jung's Psychology and Tibetan Buddhism

THE CURE OF SOULS

The "cure of souls," Jung says in his *Memories, Dreams, Reflections,* is his task.[93] Unlike most conventional psychotherapies whose goals are basically personality adjustment and cure of symptoms, and to which end manipulative therapeutic techniques are applied, Jung's psychotherapy aims at the healing of the soul, the approach to the numinous. The goal is not only the healing of pathology, but above all, the fulfillment of individual wholeness or self-realization. There is hidden in the depth of each human being a seed of all future development, which in its ultimate meaning is a seed of divinity, and the profound task of Jung's psychotherapy is to help that seed unfold and mature to its fullest potential. What are the methods that Jung developed to achieve this goal? Jung tells us that in the natural process of individuation he found a model, and a guiding principle, for his method of treatment.[94] The process of individuation is essentially an unconscious, autonomous process in which the psyche in its natural and spontaneous urge for wholeness is striving to harmonize its conscious and unconscious contents. Thus the therapist, says Jung, "must follow nature as a guide," and his or her intervention is "less a question of treatment than of developing the creative possibilities latent in the patient himself."[95]

Jung observed that those of his patients who succeeded in setting themselves free from the bondage of their life problems and achieved higher levels of psychic development and integration in essence did nothing but simply allow things to happen. They allowed their unconscious to speak to them in silence, and they listened to its messages patiently and gave them full and most serious attention. In other words, they established a conscious relationship with their unconscious processes.

> The art of letting things happen, action through inaction, letting go of oneself as told by Meister Eckhart, became for me the key that opens the door to the way. We must be able to let things happen in the psyche. For us, this is an art of which most people know nothing. Consciousness is forever interfering, helping, correcting, and negating, never leaving the psychic process to grow in peace.[96]

When the psychic process is allowed to grow in peace, the unconscious fertilizes the consciousness, and consciousness illuminates the unconscious; the interfusion and union of the two opposites result in increased awareness and a broadening of personality. Jung postulates that this can be best accomplished when the process is not regulated from the outside and the therapist does not interfere with the operation of nature. As the wider personality is being created, consciousness increases, becomes transformed, and a new center of personality emerges—the Self—while ego tendencies are diminished. The new center, like a magnet, attracts to it all that genuinely and authentically belongs to the uniqueness of personality. The integrity and unity of the individual gradually establishes itself out of its original ground plan, and all that is unessential, superfluous, superimposed, drops away. The ego that has developed in response to the pressures and dictates of the outer world, and the cultural environment, at this point bows and gives way to the pressures and urges of the individual's inner world, his inner being, his soul, the Self. Thus the ego has been sacrificed to the Self; the mundane existence has acquired a meaning, the individual has come in touch with the numinous. His initial unconscious condition has been transformed into higher consciousness, and the rounding of personality, whose symbol is the mandala, has been accomplished.

How the harmonizing of conscious and unconscious contents happens, no one knows, for it is an irrational life process. In Jung's psychotherapy there are no fixed methods of treatment; the methods naturally develop as the work progresses and in response to the needs of the particular individual. Every individual is unique and unpredictable, and therefore Jung enjoins therapists to free themselves from all preconceptions and theoretical assumptions, and abandon all methods and techniques.[97] Jung tells us he is deliberately unsystematic, and only individual understanding is the method, so to speak. "We need a different language for every patient."[98]

However, two basic methods were consistently used by Jung in his practice: work with dreams and active imagination. While dream interpretation has a long history going far back into antiquity, active imagination is the original product of Jung's artwork. Jung views the process of active imagination as equivalent to the alchemical operation. In essence it involves an ongoing dialogue between two opposites, that is, consciousness and the unconscious, in the course of which all aspects of one's being are gradually integrated. It is the work of reconciliation and union of opposites leading to psychological transformation.

There are several steps in the process. Initially the task is to induce a calm state of mind, free from thoughts, and merely to observe in a neutral way, without judgment, just to behold the spontaneous emergence and unfoldment of unconscious contents, fragments of fantasy. This part is very similar to basic meditation practices. The experience is then recorded either in a written form, or given some other tangible shape, such as a drawing, a painting, a sculpture, a dance, or any other variety of symbolic expressions.[99] In the next stage, the conscious mind begins to participate actively and deliberately in a confrontation with the unconscious. The meaning of the unconscious product and its message has to be understood and reconciled with the position and demands of the conscious mind. As Jung states:

> It is exactly as if a dialogue were taking place between two human beings with equal rights, each of whom gives the other credit for a valid argument and considers it worthwhile to modify the conflicting standpoints by means of thorough comparison and discussion or else to distinguish them clearly from one another.[100]

Finally, once the ego and the unconscious have come to terms with each other and one now has the capacity to live consciously, an ethical attitude and obligation has to follow: one no longer can conduct one's life as though unaware of the hidden workings of the unconscious.[101]

It must be stressed that the principles of Jung's psychology are not applied as a method of medical treatment but rather of self-education. Psychotherapy, says Jung,

> ...transcends its medical origins and ceases to be merely a method for treating the sick. It now treats the healthy or such as have a moral right to psychic health, whose sickness is at most the suffering that torments us all. For this reason, analytical psychology can claim to serve the common weal.[102]

In his psychotherapy Jung aims to bring about in his patients a state of fluidity in which they experience change and growth without being attached to any fixed condition. At the same time he endeavors to arouse in them a sense of their suprapersonal connections, to enlarge their capacities of awareness beyond personal consciousness.[103] This is particularly important for modern man, whose rational attitude has thwarted and repressed the spiritual dimension of life. Jung stresses that the spiritual or religious realm of experience does not refer to any creed, dogma, or metaphysical category but is a fundamental psychic function of tremendous significance.[104] He recognizes that there is no personal healing without regaining a religious outlook on life.[105]

Of central importance in therapy is the role of the psychotherapist, and the close rapport between the latter and the patient. Therapy to Jung is a dialectical process in which two psychic realities confront each other, and both must be affected and changed in the encounter.[106] The therapist, no less than the patient, cannot be immune from the experience if therapy is to be effective. Concepts are instruments of protection from experience, thanks to which the therapist can maintain a convenient distance, and besides, there is no obligation to concepts. But, as Jung says, "the spirit does not dwell in concepts."[107] Therapists equally should not shield themselves behind the screen of professional authority, for by this attitude they deprive themselves of important information gained through the channel of their unconscious.[108] At the same time, Jung is very eager to allow his patients to become psychologically mature, self-reliant, and independent from the therapist. Like the alchemist's apprentice, patients can learn "all the tricks of the laboratory" but ultimately must engage in the opus themselves for "nobody else can do it for [them]."[109] So, the endless process of individuation has to go on long after formal therapy has ended. And speaking from the standpoint of a psychotherapist, Jung tells us the encounters with the many kinds of people he met in his therapeutic work constituted for him invaluable learning experiences, and the finest and most significant interactions in his life.[110]

It is important to underline that individuation leads not only to a widening of personality, but also to a broadening of collective relationships. Contrary to the belief of some, individuation is not tantamount to isolation and abdication of social and ethical responsibilities; rather, personal consciousness and collective awareness are enhanced concurrently in a natural, spontaneous progression. The process of individuation, says Jung,

> ...brings to birth a consciousness of human community
> precisely because it makes us aware of the unconscious,
> which unites and is common to all mankind. Individua-
> tion is an at-one-ment with oneself and at the same time
> with humanity, since oneself is a part of humanity.[111]

Here we meet on the same ground the Buddhist idea of compassion, which is but the other aspect of wisdom: wisdom and compassion are the two sides of the same coin, one representing
personal and the other transpersonal consciousness, and both
equally indispensable for the attainment of enlightenment.

Finally, it must be noted that Jung's work is of such timeless
nature and limitless proportion that it is impossible, even
remotely, to convey its full flavor and meaning, and its potential
impact on an individual psyche. Furthermore, his work, along
with his life, has gone through successive stages of unfolding and
does not easily reveal itself to casual study or through focus on
only one aspect of it, and least of all by analyzing his methods.
It asks to be approached in its totality, and even then it is no easy
task to understand it.

Here is an interesting comment on this issue, by one of Jung's
disciples, Ira Progoff:

> ...I had observed...that wherever his [Jung's] theories and
> practice were taught as a specifically Jungian psychology,
> the structure of thought with its system of terms and con-
> cepts was emphasized. I recognized that one reason for
> this was that at least the terms were teachable whereas
> the *powerful direct awareness* which Jung had reached
> was not teachable....[112]

Progoff, in the course of his conversation with Jung, told him
about these thoughts. After a lengthy discussion of the issue, Progoff still restless, posed the following question to Jung:

"Suppose," I asked him, "that you were free from all the problems involved in making an intellectually valid formulation of your methods; suppose that you could state it without regard to how others would misunderstand or misuse it. Suppose that you could state it in a way that would fit your own truest feelings of it, then what would it be?..."Ach," he said..."It would be too funny. It would be a Zen touch."[113]

Progoff interprets Jung's reference to a Zen touch as meaning that his work has to be cut to the essentials, and that it has to be achieved beyond rationality.[114] Personally, I believe that Jung's reference to Zen, in all its stark simplicity, reveals more strikingly than any other elaborate comments what his dynamic method is all about.

EMANCIPATION FROM SUFFERING

Just as the "cure of souls" was Jung's task and role, suffering and emancipation from suffering, or liberation, is the ultimate goal of Buddhism. Even before the emergence of Buddhism, this was the essential problem of Indian philosophy, but it was the method that became the main and unique contribution of Buddhism to Indian philosophy. The Buddha recognized, through his own experience, and repeatedly stressed, that philosophical and metaphysical speculations and abstract thinking alone have no impact on the life of the individual. Only knowledge gained through direct experience has life-giving value. For this reason Buddha maintained the "noble silence" when asked metaphysical questions on the nature of the absolute, "the eternal truths." Instead he pointed out the way and insisted that each one of us individually must find the solutions to our fundamental existential problems, not through our intellect and logical thinking, but through development of a higher consciousness, *bodhi:* the absolute, the infinite, the numinous, is not to be conceptualized but realized within one's self. Buddha's visions and insights, the transformation of his own consciousness in the course of meditation under the bodhi tree, could not be conveyed with words. He could only show the way, the method. In its very essence the way is simple, as it is not to be looked for in hidden, faraway places, in books or sacred scriptures, but in the very depth of one's own self.[115] This is no different than the work of the alchemist's apprentice, or of Jung's patient.

When the transformation of consciousness is realized within the depth of the individual's psyche, then the metaphysical ceases to be metaphysical and is experienced as intuitive, absolute knowledge—illumination. As Lama Govinda states:

> ...what makes man blessed is not belief (in the sense of the acceptance of a definite dogma), but the becoming conscious of reality, which latter is metaphysics to us only for as long as we have not experienced it...viewed from without (as a system) Buddhism is metaphysics; viewed from within (as a form of reality) it is empiricism. In so far as "the metaphysical" is disclosed upon the path of inner experience, it was not rejected by the Buddha, it was only rejected when it was thought out upon the path of speculation. Metaphysics is an entirely relative concept, whose boundaries depend upon the respective plane of experience, upon the respective form and extent of consciousness. Buddha overcame metaphysics and its problems, not by merely ignoring them, but in an absolute positive manner, in that, through training and extension of consciousness he pushed back the boundary lines of the latter, so that the metaphysical became the empirical.[116]

Here I am reminded of Jung's statements that his work is based on empirical facts, and on the other hand, the accusation by some—who misread his work, or rather lacked the experience to understand the reality of it—that he was but a fuzzy mystic. Much of his work that was considered "mystical" has been validated by discoveries of modern science, and thus the metaphysical has become empirical.

There are many ways, many paths, leading to liberation, the goal of all schools of Buddhism. In its bare essence any path is tantamount to a radical transformation of consciousness, a symbolic death and rebirth from a profane to a spiritual mode of being. (Or, in terms of Jung's psychology, it would be the sacrifice of the ego for the emergence of the Self.)

In order to respond to the different needs and temperaments of different individuals, many methods have been developed. In tantric Buddhism especially, there is a multitude of modes and techniques. They are all designed to affect the three aspects of a human being: body, speech, and mind.

The central method, and the one that was used by Buddha himself in his transformation process, is meditation. In the tantric path, or Vajrayana, in the beginning, as preliminary practices, the various methods of meditation are followed to calm, tame, and discipline the mind, achieve one-pointed concentration, cultivate mindfulness and awareness. On this foundation a more complex method is practiced that is characteristic of the Vajrayana vehicle, namely visualization. In the act of visualization, meditators construct mental images of various degrees of complexity, representing peaceful, beautiful, and wrathful, terrifying tantric deities with whom they identify and who guide them through the process.

Each deity corresponds to a vital force within the depth of the individual, and by uniting with various deities, the meditator makes contact with those forces—positive or negative—and utilizes or rather transmutes them, to achieve higher states of consciousness. The method is based on assumptions that are irrational and can only be grasped in the way one can understand the irrational processes of life mentioned earlier in discussing Jung's method of psychotherapy.

Meditators are given a deity, chosen according to their specific needs and spiritual capacities. They are instructed to devote their fullest attention to the form of the deity that they are to create in their mind. All the minute details of the image, in all its complexity and color, are visualized to the point that it becomes just as real as the practitioners themselves. Indeed they not only contemplate the deity, they identify themselves as the deity. For a moment they have been transfigured into the divinity: the archetypal essence of it has been transferred into them. During that time of identification with the deity, they generate the so-called divine pride, pride that one is buddha.[117]

The core of visualization consists in this union with the deity. It is a dynamic process in which the meditators' ego, their ordinary consciousness, is abandoned and substituted with the higher consciousness of the deity. One could say, to use Jung's language, that the individual's ego has been sacrificed for the Self.

The process of visualization is not a matter of repressing the irrepressible parts of our psyche, the archetypal forms that unite us with all of humanity of all times, but rather to make contact with them and gradually transform them so as to achieve a higher state of consciousness. The various deities are symbols of the forces, positive and negative, good and evil, that wage a battle in our psyche. None of these forces, these energies, is lost: each is harnessed and transmuted into pure awareness, pure spiritual essence. Or, to use the alchemical language, lead is transformed into gold.

Let us look at the description of one of the deities:

Mahavajrabhairava must have a body of very deep blue color, nine faces, thirty-four arms and sixteen feet. The legs on the left side are advanced and those on the right drawn back. He is able to swallow the three worlds. He sneers and roars. His tongue is arched. He gnashes his teeth and his eyebrows are wrinkled. His eyes and his eyebrows flame like the cosmic fire at the time of the destruction of the universe. His hair is yellow and stands on end. He menaces the Gods of the material and the non-material spheres. He frightens even the terrifying deities. He roars out the word *p'ain* with a voice like the rumble of thunder. He devours flesh, marrow and human fat and drinks blood. He is crowned with five awe-inspiring skulls and is adorned with a garland made of fifteen freshly severed heads. His sacrificial cord is a black serpent. The ornaments in his ears etc. are of human bones. His belly is huge, his body naked and his penis erect. His eyebrows, eyelids, beard and body hair flame like the cosmic fire at the end of the ages. His middle face is that of a buffalo. It is horned and expresses violent anger. Above it, and between the horns, projects a yellow face.[118]

As a contrast, let us contemplate the following image:

On the disc of the autumn moon, clear and pure, you place a seed syllable. The cool blue rays of the seed syllable emanate immense cooling compassion that radiates beyond the limits of sky or space. It fulfills the needs and desires of sentient beings, bringing basic warmth so that confusions may be clarified. Then from the seed syllable you create a Mahavairocana Buddha, white in color, with the features of an aristocrat—an eight-year-old child with a beautiful, innocent, pure, powerful, royal gaze. He is dressed in the costume of a medieval king of India. He wears a glittering gold crown inlaid with wish-fulfilling jewels. Part of his long black hair floats over his shoulders and back; the rest is made into a topknot surmounted by a glittering blue diamond. He is seated crosslegged on the lunar disc with his hands in the meditation mudra holding a vajra carved from pure white crystal.[119]

And now let us contemplate a visualization, suggested by a contemporary tantric teacher, for the benefit of those devoted to Jesus Christ. It is a purification practice of body, speech, and mind.

Sit, or kneel if you like, in a comfortable position, relaxed but with your back straight. In your mind's eye, visualize Jesus before you. His face has a tranquil, peaceful, and loving expression. A picture of the resurrected Christ or of Jesus teaching may be used as a model for this visualization.

Then visualize from the crown of his head much radiant, white light coming to your own crown. This white light is in the nature of blissful energy and as it enters your body it purifies the physical contamination, or sin, accumulated over countless lifetimes. This blissful, white energy purifies all diseases of the body, including cancers, and activates and renews the functioning of your entire nervous system.

In a similar manner, a red light is visualized, radiating forth from Jesus' throat and entering your own, completely pervading your vocal center with the sensation of bliss. If you have any difficulties with your speech, always telling lies, being uncontrolled in what you say, engaging in slander, using harsh language or the like—this blissful red energy purifies you of all these negativities. As a result you discover the divine qualities of speech.

Then from Jesus' heart infinite radiant blue light comes to sink into your heart, purifying your mind of all its wrong conceptions. Your selfish and petty ego, which is like the chief or president of the delusions, and the three poisons of greed, hatred and ignorance, which are like the ego's ministers, are all purified in this blissful, blue radiance. The indecisive mind, which is especially doubtful and caught between "maybe this" and "maybe that," is clarified. Also purified is the narrow mind, which cannot see totality because its focus is too tight. As the light energy fills your mind, your heart becomes like the blue sky, embracing universal reality and all of space.[120]

With persistent practice, and as higher stages of consciousness develop, the mentally created deities assume a dynamic reality capable of affecting the meditator in a powerful way. In terms of Jung's psychology these deities in the meditator's mind become incarnated archetypes. As to their "reality" and the reason for their efficacy, we can again turn to Jung and his definition of "illusion."

By what criterion do we judge something to be an illusion? Does anything exist for the psyche that we are entitled to call illusion? What we are pleased to call illusion may be for the psyche an extremely important life-factor, something as indispensable as oxygen for the body—a psychic actuality of overwhelming significance. Presumably the psyche does not trouble itself about our categories of reality; for it, everything that *works* is real.... Nothing is more probable than that what we call illusion is very real for the psyche—for this reason we cannot take psychic reality to be commensurable with conscious reality.[121]

Of course, it should be kept in mind that in terms of Buddhist philosophy, this statement would be true on the relative level of reality only. On the ultimate level of reality everything is intrinsically void.

In the tantric *sadhanas* (spiritual exercises) the mental activity of meditation is accompanied by *mantras* and *mudras* in which speech and body take part.

Mantras are sacred sounds, auditory symbols, that have no concrete meaning but, like the sound and rhythm of music and poetry, have the power to evoke profound feelings and states of consciousness that transcend thought and ordinary speech. To the initiated, mantra speaks in a very direct, immediate way and has the capacity to call forth the dormant forces within them. To others it remains a secret. The mere recitation of a mantra without adequate preparation and the proper mental attitude is useless, for the sound of the mantra is not merely physical but above all spiritual. It has to be produced by the mind and heard by the heart.[122]

Mudras are symbolic postures and gestures in which hands and each finger participate in a most refined, elegant, and expressive manner, reminiscent of the movements of Balinese dancers. They are physical, outward expressions of inner states of being and, like the mantras when used in the proper context, are an aid to meditation, helping to incite higher states of consciousness. When all three aspects of one's being—body, speech, and mind—are simultaneously involved and harmoniously coordinated—in the performance of mudras, recitation of mantras, and deep meditation—primeval, universal forces are aroused, and the effect is thunderous. One enters another reality.

Rituals and ceremonies play a significant role in tantric practice. Prostrations, offerings of incense and flowers, chanting, *puja* (ritual worship), initiation rites, all of them have to be regarded as forms of meditation and understood for their symbolic meaning. To have their full effect, they have to be approached with a correct mental attitude and with reverence.

A typical ceremony has all the dramatic qualities of incantation and magic: it is a feast for all the senses, and it strikes at the deepest levels of one's being. There is the blast of the horns and Tibetan long trumpets, the rattle of the clapper-drums, the sound of the bells, the chanting, recitation of mantras and sacred texts, the prayer flags, the colorful robes of the lamas whose postures, gestures, and facial expressions often mirror those of the deities in the surrounding *tangkas* (sacred paintings); the fragrance of incense, flowers, ceremonial utensils, bowls with sanctified water, tea, fruit, and other delicacies. It is a spectacle and experience that cannot be described, but neither can it ever be forgotten.

The Spiritual Friend and the Analyst

Since liberation cannot be attained by way of books or abstract knowledge but only through experience, the need for a human guru, or spiritual teacher, is of tremendous importance. Only with the help and guidance of another human being can one's consciousness be awakened and real progress made. But this other human being must be a teacher who is qualified and who him- or herself is far along the path. His conduct, his knowledge, the clarity of his mind, his wisdom and compassion must be such that he can serve not only as a teacher but as a living example of the enlightened attitude. Gurus cannot magically transfer their wisdom to the disciples, but their words, which resonate beyond the meaning of the ordinary words, can touch and move the disciples when they are ready for the teaching. When that happens it is as if a key has opened the door of perception in the innermost being of the disciples, and gradually their horizons are widened. It feels literally that consciousness, the light, is expanding at each contact with the guru. The human guru, being the model of a complete person, is but the archetypal symbol of the supreme guru, or the principle of buddhahood, and so the process goes on in the minds of the disciples till the image of the guru has been integrated within themselves. The disciple realizes that the teacher is not outside but inside his psyche, and is none other than his own Self.

The function of gurus, who are sometimes also called spiritual friends, has many aspects. Let us look at the imaginative text of the eleventh-century Tibetan teacher and philosopher Gampopa, describing the role of spiritual friends.

> The "similes" are that spiritual friends are like a guide when we travel in unknown territory, an escort when we pass through dangerous regions and a ferry-man when we cross a great river.
>
> As to the first, when we travel guideless in an unknown

territory there is the danger of going astray and getting lost. But if we go with a guide then there is no such danger, and without missing a single step we reach the desired place....

In the second simile dangerous regions are haunted by thieves and robbers, wild beasts and other noxious animals. When we go there without an escort, there is the danger of losing our body, life or property; but when we have a strong escort we reach the desired place without loss....

Finally in the third simile when we cross the great river, if we have boarded a boat without a boatman, we are either drowned or carried away by the current and do not reach the other shore; but if there is a boatman we land safely by his efforts.[123]

Jung knew well of the dangers of the "wild beasts and other noxious animals" and the terror when plunging into the dark regions of one's unconscious, as he experimented with these himself. And so did the alchemists before him. They were also fully aware of the potential psychic explosion inherent in their *opus*. No doubt, both the alchemists and Jung would be in full agreement with the warnings of the Tibetan teacher.

Following in the footsteps of Shakyamuni Buddha in never imposing his teachings on others, it is part of the Tibetan tradition that instruction should be given only in response to a sincere request and serious intent. Tibetan teachers believe that the very act of seeking and requesting help creates the proper energy that is conducive to receiving it, and listening not only with ears but with the heart as well.[124]

The analyst plays essentially the same role as the spiritual friend; yet there is an important distinction. As stated earlier, Jung postulates that in the course of psychological treatment, the therapist must be equally affected by the therapeutic encounter. This may become an experience of renewal for the therapist, but on the other hand may also result in psychological contamination, threatening the therapist's own emotional balance. The guru, by contrast, one is told, having attained high spiritual realization, is immune to such contamination and cannot be affected by his students' negativities. In fact some meditation practices in Tibetan Buddhism include a mental offering to the guru consisting of all objects of one's greed and hatred, in brief, all negativities. At the same time I have been told by the lamas that the responses of their students—and particularly the recognition that they helped clear confusion and reduce suffering—do affect them and add to the store of their energies.

4 Archetypal Symbols

As discussed in the previous chapter, visualization is one of the main meditation methods in the Vajrayana. The different types of deities visualized in personified form are expressed outwardly in tantric iconography, while inwardly they correspond to different psychological states. By identifying with the various deities of the Tibetan Buddhist pantheon, the profane consciousness is transcended into the knowledge of the holy, and thus images become symbols of transformation. The anthropomorphic tantric images are regarded as archetypes yet become real to the meditator. According to Jung, archetypes *come to life* when they are meaningful to an individual.[125] Like all powerful symbols, tantric images, when infused with emotion, gain numinosity and supply meditators with energy that carry them a step forward into another psychological realm—the transpersonal, spiritual.

What is the role of images in the practice of Buddhism, whose philosophical and metaphysical foundations are based on the concept of emptiness? In the words of Lama Govinda:

The abstractness of philosophical concepts and conclusions requires to be constantly corrected by direct experience, by the practice of meditation and the contingencies of daily life. The anthropomorphic element in the Vajrayana is therefore not born from a lack of intellectual understanding (as in the case of primitive man), but, on the contrary, from the conscious desire to penetrate from a merely intellectual and theoretical attitude to the direct awareness of reality. This cannot be achieved through building up convictions, ideals, and aims based on reasoning, but only through conscious penetration of those layers of our mind which cannot be reached or influenced by logical arguments and discursive thought.

Such penetration and transformation is only possible through the compelling power of inner vision, whose primordial images or "archetypes" are the formative principles of our mind. Like seeds they sink into the fertile soil of our subconsciousness in order to germinate, to grow and to unfold their potentialities....

The subjectivity of inner vision does not diminish its reality-value. Such visions are not hallucinations, because their reality is that of the human psyche. They are symbols, in which the highest knowledge and the noblest endeavor of the human mind are embodied. Their visualization is the creative process of spiritual projection, through which inner experience is translated into visible form, comparable to the creative act of an artist, whose subjective idea, emotion, or vision, is transformed into an objective work of art, which now takes on a reality of its own, independent of its creator.[126]

Similarly Jung tells us that archetypes initially are empty forms but contain the possibility of certain perceptions and actions, and when activated they become a powerful force in the life and behavior of an individual.[127] Indeed, the archetype may take an autonomous reality of its own and take control over the entire personality. The vision may lead to artistic creations or scientific discoveries, like the famous case of Kekule's discovery of the benzene ring.[128] But the visions can also lead to insanity if they are not integrated into consciousness. The dividing line between the two roads is frequently very thin.

Tibetan Buddhists, as well as Jung, are aware of the dangers involved and therefore urge that proper safeguards be taken.

Tantric visualization, and the somewhat comparable active imagination technique of Jung, both require guidance of a qualified teacher, or analyst. Furthermore, in Vajrayana practice every visualization is preceded and terminated by meditation on emptiness and dissolution of images, which acts as a protection against continued identification with the symbols: the meditator is made aware that the deities are products of imagination.

One of the most important (and in Tibet the most popular) deities is Tara. She is the feminine aspect of the Buddha. In Tibet she is revered as the mother of all buddhas. Tara, in her essence, symbolizes the totally developed wisdom that transcends reason. She is the buddha of enlightened activity, the liberator who, by releasing one from the bondage of egocentric passions, leads from the shores of profane worldly involvement (samsara) to the other shore of illumination (nirvana). Tara appears in a variety of aspects: the green Tara, red Tara, white Tara, etc., twenty-one of them, and each corresponding to slightly different archetypal images in the psyche. In Jungian terminology she represents the Mother archetype. However, she is the image of the mother who has integrated in herself all the opposites, positive and negative. Thus to Erich Neumann (a disciple of Jung), Tara symbolizes the highest form, the culmination of the feminine archetype. She is "the Great Goddess who, in the totality of her unfolding, fills the world from its lowest elementary phase to its supreme spiritual transformation."[129]

Besides peaceful and wrathful deities, another category of "beings" plays an important role in Tibetan Buddhism. They are the so-called *dakinis* who have divine or demonic qualities and can represent the human inspirational impulse. They are female embodiments of knowledge and magic powers and are described as "genii of meditation and spiritual helpers," capable of awakening the dormant forces hidden in the darkness of the unconscious.

The word *dakini*, or in Tibetan, *khandroma*, means "space" and "ether," referring to that which makes movement possible.[130]

One gets the feeling of the fluid nature of a dakini; she moves the psyche and causes it to liquefy all that is rigid and concrete, whatever is encapsulated in conceptual thoughts and dogmas, any fixed formulation. In that sense she symbolizes the principle of motion and reflects the dynamic forces that are the same in the cosmos as in the psyche of the individual.

The dakini of the highest rank is Vajrayogini. She is the divine figure of the inspiring muse who "redeems the treasures of aeons of experience, which lie dormant in the subconscious, and raises them into the realm of higher consciousness, beyond that of our intellect."[131] Tibetan Buddhists say that Vajrayogini has always existed deep within ourselves, in our unconscious, but is suffocated by the ego. When the concept of the ego is pierced, we allow Vajrayogini to appear. (When I think of Vajrayogini I am always reminded of the Sleeping Beauty.) Vajrayogini in Tibetan iconography is depicted with a curious expression that is simultaneously loving and smiling, but also wrathful, thus revealing the essential ambivalence of every archetype.

In the context of Jung's psychology, Vajrayogini would be a primordial image, and as such can act as a mediator, "proving its redeeming power, a power it has always possessed in various religions."[132]

The tantric symbol of dakini has been sometimes compared in the West with Jung's concept of one of the major archetypes, namely, the *anima*.[133] The anima is usually referred to as the female aspect of the male psyche. It appears in many different forms and has both benevolent and demonic aspects. She can be a guide and mediator, leading a man to his transformation—or to his doom.

But the notion of anima is much more complex. First of all, anima does not apply exclusively to a man's psyche: as an archetypal figure she can function in the psyche of either gender. In the male-oriented Western world, the concept of anima, as the feminine counterpart of the masculine psyche, and the proper integration of the two aspects, is crucial to the psychological balance of the individual and the culture. In the Eastern world, on the other hand, the feminine quality, the *yin,* as well as the *yang,* the masculine quality, the goddess as well as the god, have been integral parts of the culture. There could be no god without a goddess; one is unthinkable without the other. The most prevalent image in tantric iconography is the symbol of *yab-yum,* the god and goddess, father and mother, in ecstatic embrace, symbolizing the perfect union of the masculine and feminine elements, the union of opposites, which is the fundamental inner experience.

Jung is right when he says that the concept of anima as he stated it is lacking in the Eastern view.[134] It should be added that it is the notion of anima as he formulated it in his earlier writings, and as it is most commonly understood. In the East that concept would be superfluous. Anima, however, can be the bridge to the Self. As such, she has a definite correspondence to the dakini, the ethereal being who is both the essence and the carrier of wisdom. In that sense dakinis, and actually all tantric deities, peaceful and wrathful, divine and demonic, can be looked at as messengers and personifications of supreme wisdom, and therefore they function as catalysts in the process of integration. Or, to put it differently, they are numinous personalities, embodiments of archetypes, expressing different attributes of the Self.

A dakini may at times have a correspondence to the archetype of the anima, but may also just as well be the equivalent of the archetype of the "wise old man," who represents superior insight. And just as the image of Philemon, the "wise old man," appeared to Jung and seemed quite real to him, similarly a deity appears real to the meditator. The difference is, however, that the dakini, or deity, is not a spontaneous appearance, as Jung's vision of Philemon was. It is instead a deity that the guru bestows on the student during initiation to facilitate his or her progress, and it is chosen in accordance with the individual's specific needs, characteristics, and capacities. Such a deity is called *yidam* and becomes the student's guardian and mentor—the "wise old man." It has been said that a dakini "provides hidden intimations from deeper layers of one's being."[135] Here the dakini would reflect the quality of the anima, which Jung describes as a personification of the unconscious,[136] and having the connective qualities of Eros.[137]

But once again, it should be emphasized that all these anthropomorphic images of the tantric pantheon—deities, dakinis, yidams—are not identified as external beings, but are none other than the reflections of the individual's mind, and are revealed in inward experiences. Therefore, the various archetypal figures can appear in one form or another at different times and under different circumstances. The goal is to make contact with these psychic realities and bring them to consciousness—or, as Jung would say, to bring them into our own souls. Jung recognized that religious function is not a matter of faith and outward form that leaves the soul utterly barren; it is rooted in the human psyche and yearns for expression but can be discovered only through one's own direct experience. Thus Jung states:

> With a truly tragic delusion...theologians fail to see that it is not a matter of proving the existence of the light, but of blind people who do not know that their eyes could see. It is high time we realize that it is pointless to praise the light and preach it if nobody can see it. It is much more needful to teach people the art of seeing. For it is obvious that far too many people are incapable of establishing a connection between the sacred figures and their own psyche; they cannot see to what extent the equivalent images are lying dormant in their own unconscious.[138]

To Jung it is evident that the solution to this problem—developing the capacity for inner vision and experiencing the *magnum mysterium*, the cosmic reality—can be achieved only by making contact with the psyche. In other words, the psyche, or the mind, as Tibetan Buddhists would say, is the vehicle of transformation.

The sacred images—whether those of the Tibetan pantheon or the modern world, or of any mythology of any time and place—are the common heritage of humanity and are present in every individual. And Jung found out in his therapeutic practice that contemporary men and women in the Western world spontaneously produced, from their unconscious, images that were part of mythologies of remote places and ancient times, and that these images could have a profound and powerful effect on the individual. In the act of vision, of contact with the symbol, they could be renewed and their psychic energy transformed, a fact Tibetan Buddhists have known for centuries.

As mentioned earlier, Jung's particular approach to psychotherapy went beyond goals and methods as traditionally understood and practiced; to him psychotherapy is ultimately an approach to the numinous. It is on this ground that Jung and tantra meet; they penetrate and transform the same psychic realities.

The process of individuation, or psychological development, leads progressively further away from the ego to the Self, from the unconscious to consciousness, from the personal to the transpersonal, the holy, the realization that the macrocosm is being mirrored in the microcosm of the human psyche.

The task is the redemption of the Self, the psychic totality, the lapis, "the great treasure that lies hidden in the cave of the unconscious,"[139] personified in the Buddha, in Vajrayogini, the Sleeping Beauty, suffocated by the ego. And the task can be accomplished, according to Jung, when the archetypal symbol, the Self, is made conscious and is disengaged from the unconscious identification with the ego. In other words, the Self, God, the Buddha, Vajrayogini has to be redeemed by human consciousness. This is the ultimate goal of psychological development in the framework of Jung's psychotherapy.

The notion that matter, symbolizing the temporal reality of the ego, is hiding God was part of a Gnostic myth, and also the underlining theme in alchemy.[140] The alchemical, in contrast to the Christian work of redemption, is an active endeavor that is remarkably similar to the Buddhist approach. In alchemy, says Jung, "man takes upon himself the duty of carrying out the redeeming *opus*, and attributes the state of suffering and consequent need of redemption to the *anima mundi* imprisoned in matter."[141]

But the work of redemption, whether in alchemy, tantra, or Jung, cannot be left to nature; it requires conscious effort. Above all it must be a living experience, it must take place in the midst of life. The alchemists believed that "the substance that harbors the divine secret is everywhere...even in the most loathsome filth."[142] Tantric Buddhists similarly believe that every event and situation, good or evil, can become a vehicle of spiritual transformation. Nothing is to be rejected. And Jung's psychology too welcomes every aspect of the psyche, rejects no part of it, and seeks it in the depth and the height, darkness and light, and in simple outer and inner events of everyday life.

THE TIBETAN BOOK OF THE DEAD

In his "Psychological Commentary on *The Tibetan Book of the Dead*," or *Bardo Tödöl,* Jung states that this work has been "my constant companion, and to it I owe not only many stimulating ideas and discoveries, but also many fundamental insights."[143] *The Tibetan Book of the Dead* is ostensibly about death and dying, with instructions to the soul of the departed during forty-nine days of peregrination until new birth.

In a modern commentary, basically addressed to the Western world, Chögyam Trungpa Rinpoche calls it "The Tibetan Book of Birth," thereby making the point that birth and death are fundamental principles that recur constantly in this life.[144] The meaning of the word *bardo* is derived from *bar,* which means "in between," and *do,* which means "island" or "mark." It is therefore "a sort of landmark which stands between two things,"[145] and it refers to an intermediate state, a period of transition. We recognize here the idea of the intermediary, twilight level of consciousness or the twilight period at sunset or dawn, when day turns into night or vice versa. These are borderline states; they are times of crisis, when the tension is at its peak, but they are also the most pregnant psychologically, since they are times when change can most readily occur. Inherent in such states is the opportunity for transformation. In the crack between two worlds—of the living and the dead, of death and rebirth—lies the supreme opportunity. According to the *Tibetan Book of the Dead*, it is at the moment immediately following death that the mind is capable of attaining liberation. At that moment one reaches the subtlest level of consciousness, the clear-light mind, but because one is not familiar with it, one misses the opportunity to use it to gain enlightenment and instead descends progressively back into the world of the unconscious and a new birth, when the wheel of samsara and suffering starts all over again. In its journey through the underworld, the mind encounters at first beautiful, peaceful, and later frightening, wrathful deities. The teaching of the *Book* is that these deities are but projections of the mind that need to be recognized as such, that is, as empty forms and illusory images. The confusion is then transformed into transcendental wisdom.

In his commentary, Jung asks us to read the *Bardo Tödöl* backward. Looking at it that way, it would appear like the course of the individuation process: from the darkness of the unconscious to the clear light at the end. By contrast, the clear light is experienced at the very onset in the journey through the *bardo*. The path of ascent or descent of awareness is reversed in the Tibetan and Jungian approaches. But to the Buddhist, this would be one and the same, since there is no beginning or end. This may be a problem to Westerners, for it relates to one of the major conceptual differences between Eastern and Western modes of thinking, namely that the West perceives time as linear, whereas in the East time is cyclical—there is the eternal return. Thus, while the West produced the *Divine Comedy,* the journey of the soul's ascent, the East produced the *Bardo Tödöl*, the path of the mind's descent.

To Jung it was self-evident that "the whole book is created out of the archetypal contents of the unconscious." The world of gods and spirits, according to him, is the collective unconscious within us.[146] By introducing this book to the Western world, Jung acknowledged its high psychological significance, its remarkable understanding of the phenomenon of projection, and its philosophical implications: the transitoriness of the phenomenal, relative world, and the permanence of the eternal absolute reality. Through his commentary he made the *Book* as relevant to contemporary Westerners as it was to the remote and secluded society of Tibet centuries ago.

Today, in a somewhat different manner, Trungpa Rinpoche throws light on the significance of the *Bardo Tödöl* and looks at it from another standpoint. He interprets the experience of *bardo* in terms of the six realms of existence in Buddhist mythology— the realms of: hell, the hungry ghost, the animal, the human, the jealous gods, and the gods—and relates them to corresponding aspects of our psychological states. The realm of hell is the state of anger, which becomes self-destructive. The hungry ghost realm is the condition of insatiable hunger for possessions. The animal realm represents the absence of mystery; it is the world of security and comfort, predictable and mechanical. The human realm is the world of passion and unceasing pursuit of pleasure and wealth. The realm of the jealous gods is the world of paranoia and intrigue. Finally, the realm of the gods is the state of pride and narcissism, intoxication with one's ego.[147]

All these realms are portraits of this world of samsara, of frustration and suffering. In the deities the soul meets, we recognize our familiar gods of daily living, who haunt us and affect us all the time if we do not acknowledge them. That means we must become conscious of them, integrate them, and develop an ethical attitude if we are to live complete and meaningful lives. Otherwise, as with the visions in the journey through the bardo, we can go progressively deeper into the unconscious until we reach the total darkness, the point of no return.

The Mandala

The mandala, the mystic circle, is a very important and significant symbol in Tibetan Buddhism. It is one of the most ancient
symbols, which according to Jung can be traced to Paleolithic
time[148] and can be found in all places and all ages. The most elaborate and artistic mandalas have been created by Tibetan Buddhists. They are images containing symbols of opposites grouped
around a central nucleus, and their structure and design express
both the world projected outside and the inner world of the psyche. Thus to the disciple they reveal the interplay of forces that
operate in the cosmos and within his own mind.

The Tibetan mandalas are not mere aesthetic compositions;
they are religious and philosophical symbols with precise mean-
ings fixed by tradition. We are told that

> every detail in them is significant and does not depend
> on arbitrary moods or whims of an artist, but is the out-
> come of centuries of meditative experience and a con-
> ventional language of symbols as precise as the sign
> language of mathematical formulas, where not only each
> sign, but also its position within the formula determines
> its value.[149]

In other words, here mandalas have been born out of visions and
interior experiences of highly advanced meditators and in a very
special, spiritually creative environment.

Jung, on the other hand, through his personal experiences
and in his work with patients had observed the same motif of
the mandala occurring spontaneously when the psyche is in a
process of reintegration following a time of disequilibrium. In
those instances the authors of mandalas could not possibly have
had any knowledge of Tibetan Buddhism. Jung saw that in his
schizophrenic patients, "mandala symbols appear very frequently
in moments of psychic disorientation as compensatory ordering

factors. This aspect is expressed above all in their mathematical structure."[150] He concluded that the mandala is an archetype of order, of psychic integration and wholeness, and appears as a natural attempt at self-healing. But it was in the dreams and active imagination of his patients who were on their journey to individuation that Jung found most surprising evidences of the formation of mandalas. The contents of these visions express in a symbolic way the violent clashes of opposites and their eventual reconciliation when the Self emerges at the center of the psyche and is represented by an innermost point. The harmony that is then established has a numinous quality.

In tantric Buddhism the disciples, after being initiated, are given specific instructions on how to visualize the mandala, which portrays the peaceful and wrathful deities, the clashing forces of existence, the primordial impulses and passions, as well as the spark of divinity—all lying in the depths of the psyche. By mentally entering the mandalas, they explore the gross and subtle workings of their minds, their unconscious, and gradually approach their own innermost nuclear center, where all opposites are united. The whole process is expressed by means of complex symbols, recapitulating the drama of psychic fragmentation, disintegration, and reintegration: from duality, multiplicity, psychic fragmentation after the primeval unconscious oneness, to psychic reintegration, nonduality, pure consciousness.

Despite the infinite variety of mandalas, whether produced by tantric meditators or in the dreams and active imagination of Jung's patients or by individuals anywhere in the world, we find in them a fundamental conformity of pattern, for they originate in the collective unconscious, common to all humanity. They are symbols of unity, reconciling opposites on a higher level of consciousness. At the same time, they are a means of expression of a universal reality, and by being expressed and contacted, they produce profound effects inducing transformative experiences. In the mandala motif, Jung saw "one of the best examples of the universal operation of an archetype."[151]

5 Connections, Similarities, Differences

INTRODUCTION

In this chapter I propose first to discuss the conceptual and methodological equivalents between the two systems and identify the points where they meet, where they are similar or parallel, and where they differ. Next, I will examine Jung's view of Eastern traditions in terms of their relevance to the Western world, and his as well as the Tibetan Buddhists' view regarding the possible dangers inherent in practicing tantra. Finally, I should like to comment on the issues of ethics and their potential impact on the world community, which are an important and integral aspect of both systems.

CONSCIOUSNESS AND THE UNCONSCIOUS

The basic concepts of consciousness and the unconscious in the Jungian system and in Buddhism have a variety of connotations and therefore are subject to much misunderstanding and distortions. To compound the problem, Jung's concepts are often confused with those of Freud, which are vastly different. I shall try to review some of them, being well aware that my survey is grossly inadequate. A whole lifetime—or as Buddhists would say, several lives—of study and practice would hardly enable anyone to comprehend fully these concepts in both systems.

Jung views consciousness and the unconscious as being of

equal importance.[152] Consciousness, however, is a "late-born descendant of the unconscious psyche,"[153] which means that the former emerges out of the latter. In one instance Jung equates consciousness with ego.[154] He postulates that:

> Consciousness needs a center, an ego to which something is conscious. We know of no other kind of consciousness, nor can we imagine a consciousness without an ego. There can be no consciousness when there is no one to say: "I am conscious."[155]

Jung believes that consciousness, "that most remarkable of all of nature's curiosities," exists and has an urge to be widened for the simple reason that without it "things go less well."[156] On the other hand Jung talks about "higher consciousness," which is a deeper and more receptive consciousness that relates to the transpersonal realm.

And in paraphrasing a sentence by Ignatius Loyola, putting it into psychological terminology, Jung states:

> Man's consciousness was created to the end that it may (1) recognize...its descent from a higher unity...; (2) pay due and careful regard to this source...; (3) execute its commands intelligently and responsibly...; and (4) thereby afford the psyche as a whole the optimum degree of life and development.[157]

According to Jung, the symbols of wholeness, which resolve and transcend opposites, could be called "consciousness,"as well as "self," "higher ego," or anything else. To him, "all these terms are simply names for the facts that alone carry weight."[158]

The development and extension of the sphere of consciousness is what Jung calls individuation.[159] But he postulates that the conscious mind occupies only a relatively central position while the unconscious psyche surrounds it.[160]

The unconscious is the psychic area with an unlimited scope. It is the "matrix of all potentialities,"[161] and it is best imagined as a fluid state that has a life of its own, and whose activity is autonomous and independent. "The unconscious perceives, has purposes and intuitions, feels and thinks as does the conscious mind."[162] Jung defines the contents of the unconscious as follows:

> ...everything of which I know, but of which I am not at the moment thinking; everything of which I was once conscious but have now forgotten; everything perceived by my senses, but not noted by my conscious mind; everything which, involuntarily and without paying attention to it, I feel, think, remember, want, and do; all the future things that are taking shape in me and will sometime come to consciousness....[163]

Thus the unconscious includes future contents of the conscious psyche and anticipates future conscious processes. But in addition, the unconscious contains ancestral deposits accumulated since immemorial time. To Jung, therefore, the unconscious has a Janus face: one side of it points back to prehistory, the world of raw instincts, and its other side points toward man's future fate.[164] This is a paradox, for "the unconscious is seen as a creative factor, even as a bold innovator, and yet it is at the same time the stronghold of ancestral conservatism."[165] Like Mercurius—the personification of the unconscious—it is dualistic and contains all aspects of human nature: dark and light, evil and good, bestial and superhuman, demonic and divine.[166] One can conceive of the unconscious as a treasure-house that is the source of all inspiration, creativity, and wisdom. As an autonomous psychic system, which speaks in the language of symbols, one of its roles is to correct the biases of the conscious mind and compensate its one-sidedness with a broader, imaginal, nonrational perception that restores the balance and reveals a more comprehensive meaning. Unconscious motives are often wiser and more objective than conscious thinking. Therefore the unconscious may be a valuable guide pointing the way to one's true destination, a destination that is true to one's self and not falsified by prejudices of the conscious mind.

At the basis of separate individual consciousness and the unconscious behind them, there is the collective unconscious, the common heritage of all humanity and the universal source of all conscious life. In the depth of the collective unconscious, there are no individual or cultural differences, no separation. It is the realm of primordial unity, nonduality, and through it each person is connected with the rest of humanity.

Tibetan Buddhists say that the conscious mind when it is clear, unobscured, free from projections—the pure consciousness—is the root of happiness and liberation, and is experienced as a state of bliss. This is the highest state of consciousness known as clear light. However, there are various kinds and degrees of consciousness, and they are described in different terms. Similarly, there are various levels of consciousness and the unconscious in the structure of the psyche as conceptualized by Jung.

In the view of one school of Buddhist tenets, there are six kinds of consciousness: those of sight, hearing, smell, taste, touch, and the mental consciousness. On top of these six is the afflicted, or deluded, consciousness responsible for the misconception of the ego. And underlying all of it is the "storehouse consciousness" *(alaya-vijnana)*, the source of all consciousness, where all one's experiences since beginningless time are stored. Its latent contents appear to the other kinds of consciousness when aroused by the corresponding conditions and associations.[167]

The notion of storehouse consciousness clearly corresponds to Jung's concept of the unconscious. Like Jung's description of the unconscious, Lama Govinda argues that *alaya-vijnana*

...contains demonic as well as divine qualities, cruelty as well as compassion, egotism as well as selflessness, delusion as well as knowledge, blind passion and darkest drives as well as profound longing for light and liberation.[168]

And in discussing the tantric experience Lama Govinda states:

> It is not sufficient to identify ourselves with the oneness of a common origin or a potential Buddhahood, unless we take the decisive step toward the transformation and reintegration of the divergent tendencies or elements of our psyche.[169]

When we try to compare, as Jung did, the Buddhist concept of enlightened mind with the collective unconscious or the higher consciousness, we encounter enormous obstacles due to the fact that all these concepts have many different aspects, and are ambiguous and controversial. Furthermore, we are dealing here with two different categories: philosophical and metaphysical on one hand, and psychological on the other hand, and consequently no real comparison could be made. Yet, in either system, Buddhist or Jung's, these categories represent only abstract knowledge, and do not and cannot express the profound experience that is the aim of both, namely individual transformation achieved by transcending the mundane existence, and thereby attaining liberation or self-realization. In that moment of transcendence the knowledge ceases to be philosophical or psychological: it is the indescribable, direct, immediate knowledge beyond words and thoughts, the experience of the void *(shunyata)*, the numinous, the Self, oneness of human and divine.

Jung referred to this experience, in one way or another, through much of his writings, but he articulated it most eloquently in his "Septem Sermones ad Mortuos"—Seven Sermons to the Dead—written during the period of his confrontation with the unconscious. This brief but extraordinary work, replete with paradoxes, is strikingly reminiscent of Buddhist thinking. In fact it echoes the words of *The Heart Sutra,* "form is emptiness,

emptiness is form," or the statement from *The Lankavatara Sutra* that "space is form, and...as space penetrates into form, form is space."[170] This is how Jung puts it:

> Nothingness is the same as fullness. In infinity full is no better than empty. Nothingness is both empty and full.... A thing that is infinite and eternal hath no qualities, since it hath all qualities.[171]

Jung names this nothingness or fullness *pleroma,*[172] which he distinguishes from *creatura,* the principle of distinctiveness. In pleroma "both thinking and being cease, since the eternal and infinite possess no qualities.... In the pleroma there is nothing and everything."[173] And in a further passage Jung writes:

> Everything that discrimination taketh out of the pleroma is a pair of opposites. To god, therefore, always belongeth the devil.
>
> This inseparability is as close and, as your own life hath made you see, as indissoluble as the pleroma itself. Thus it is that both stand very close to the pleroma, in which all opposites are extinguished and joined.[174]

One recognizes in pleroma the Buddhist concept of emptiness, as well as the most important tantric concept of polarity and its integration, which is at the very heart of every Vajrayana meditative practice. At the same time Jung's concept of the "transcendent function" is a development and practical application of the principle of pleroma. It should be noted that Jung wrote "Septem Sermones ad Mortuos" at the time when he had not yet discovered the Eastern traditions.

SPIRITUAL TRANSFORMATION

The ultimate goal of Jung's psychology and of Tibetan Buddhism is spiritual transformation. Jung refers to it as self-realization, wholeness, while for Tibetan Buddhists it is buddhahood, enlightenment, for the sake of all beings. According to the latter, every single individual has the potential to become a buddha, to achieve the supreme transformation. The desire for light, for a higher consciousness, according to the Buddhists as well as Jung, has been always present and is ubiquitous. As Jung says:

> ...within the soul from its primordial beginnings there has been a desire for light and an irrepressible urge to rise out of the primal darkness...the psychic primal night...is the same today as it has been for countless millions of years. The longing for light is the longing for consciousness.[175]

For the Buddhist there is aspiration toward buddhahood, which is man's quintessential nature, and for Jung it is the urge toward wholeness. In both instances it entails a long, and for Jung a never-ending journey, which is unique to each individual and which can be accomplished only in the mind. In tantric Buddhism in particular, the mind is the king whose power is unlimited. Just like the alchemist who can change metal into gold, the mind can transform any event into transcendental wisdom and use it as a means to attain enlightenment. And that majestic power lies within us, nowhere else, and not apart from us, but to recognize it we need the key of consciousness.

According to the teaching of tantric Buddhism, enlightenment can be attained in the present life. It consists of a fundamental change in our perception of reality, "the turning about in the deepest seat of consciousness," when the "I" or self-consciousness has turned its attention toward the universal consciousness. It is the "intuitive experience of the infinite and the all-embracing oneness of all that is."[176] The experience can also be described as a discovery of a world beyond the ordinary world of appearances, in which all opposites no longer exist. In this open space, one abandons all limitations; there is no exclusiveness, no this or that, but this and that; everything is included, nothing rejected. This is the world of nonduality, pleroma, from which everything originates, and into which everything disappears. Buddhists call it shunyata, emptiness, the open space that contains the principles of both causality and synchronicity.

> In its deepest metaphysical sense, it [emptiness] is the primordial ground, the ever-present starting point of all creation. It is the principle of unlimited potentiality.... On the intellectual plane *sunyata* is the relativity of all things and conditions, insofar as no thing exists independently but only in relationship to others—and ultimately in relationship to the whole universe. This relationship is more than a mere causal, time-space relationship; it is one of a common ground and a simultaneous presence of all factors of existence....[177]

From the tantric point of view each being contains the whole universe. There is no separation of the individual and universal mind, the mind not being subject to time and space limitation. Today the discoveries of modern physics reveal the basic view of the world as one of unity, interrelation, and interpenetration of all things and events.[178] And according to the *Avatamsaka Sutra,*

> All the Buddha-lands and all the Buddhas themselves, are manifested in my own being....[179]

This parallels Jung's conviction that the macrocosm manifests itself in the microcosm of the human psyche. He talks about

> ...that unknown quantity in man which is as universal and wide as the world itself, which is in him by nature and cannot be acquired. Psychologically, this corresponds to the collective unconscious....[180]

The collective unconscious is the realm of the psyche where nonduality prevails, but which contains, like emptiness, the principle of unlimited potentiality. Thus to Jung the principles of the universe are reflected in the psyche.

THE UNION OF OPPOSITES

The fundamental concept in tantra is recognition of polarity, and its integration is the core of tantric practice: the union of male and female energies, matter and spirit, active and passive principles, wisdom, the discriminating principle (personified by Manjushri, the buddha of wisdom), and compassion, the unifying principle (personified by Avalokiteshvara, the buddha of compassion).

The principle of opposites is equally of primary importance in Jung's psychology. For Jung, opposition is inherent in the structure of the psyche, as it is in the cosmos: the cosmological is reflected on the psychological level. Within the framework of his psychology, the basic pair of opposites are consciousness and the unconscious. One could say that on the cosmological level, the former represents creatura, individuality, and the latter pleroma, nonduality.

On the psychological level, the significance of the principle of opposites lies in the fact that the psyche is a dynamic unity, a self-regulating system in which consciousness and the unconscious are complementary to each other. To deny one or the other results in one-sidedness, disequilibrium, and hence a loss of wholeness. "There must always be a high and low, hot and cold, etc.," says Jung. However, "the point is not conversion into the opposite but conservation of previous values together with recognition of their opposites."[181] Nothing is rejected, and nothing is accepted as an absolute. In Jung's view:

It is...a fundamental mistake to imagine that when we see the non-value in a value or the untruth in the truth, the value or the truth ceases to exist. It has only become *relative*. Everything human is relative because everything rests on an inner polarity....[182]

To Jung *"the union of opposites through the middle path"* is a "most fundamental item of inward experience."[183] The resolution of opposites ends conflict and brings wholeness. But wholeness cannot be achieved through suppression or negation, which is always one-sided, but only by raising one's standpoint to a higher level of consciousness. This is the basic premise of Jung's psychological method. "Individuation, or becoming whole," he says "is neither a *summum bonum* nor a *summum desideratum,* but the painful experience of the union of opposites."[184] I should like to suggest though, that the realization of the union of opposites *is* the *summum bonum* because it brings with it spiritual freedom, experienced in the integrated and unified personality.

Buddha on his journey to enlightenment abandoned asceticism, as he must have realized that by practicing it one rejects part of oneself and consequently wholeness cannot be attained. Instead he adopted and later taught the middle way.

THE MIDDLE WAY AND THE MADHYAMAKA

Buddha's way, the middle way, was reformulated and systematized in philosophical terms by the third-century Indian philosopher Nagarjuna in his Madhyamaka (Middle Way) system of thought, which is considered the central philosophy of Mahayana Buddhism. While Buddha maintained his "noble silence" when asked philosophical and metaphysical questions, Nagarjuna, a brilliant dialectician, applied the dialectic method and argued that truth is not to be found in any view or concept, in any system of understanding. The truth, the absolute, which is inexpressible, can only be comprehended in rising above any kind of exclusiveness. The conflict produced by reason and contending positions can be resolved by attaining a higher standpoint—

that is, by the awareness of the total rather than the separate parts. One goes beyond to intuition, considered to be a higher faculty: the nondual knowledge, the knowledge of the Real, the Absolute.

And here is Jung's view of intuition:

> In intuition a content presents itself whole and complete, without our being able to explain or discover how this content came into existence.... Intuitive knowledge possesses an intrinsic certainty and conviction....[185]

The central point in the philosophy of Nagarjuna is the rule of the middle way, which in practice means: "to see things as they are, to recognize the possibility of determining things differently from different standpoints and to recognize that these determinations cannot be seized as absolute."[186]

Equally basic to the philosophy of Nagarjuna is the distinction between the mundane and ultimate truth, which is actually one of the foundations of Buddha's teaching, and is always emphasized in Mahayana Buddhism. But this does not mean a separation between the worldly and the transcendental. It is rather the realization of the relativity of the mundane, and a consequent deepening of inward awareness in the process of which the mundane, the superficial, is not destroyed but is transformed and then seen in a new light.[187]

The Madhyamaka teaches that

> ...to realize the ultimate is not to abandon the mundane but to learn to see it "with the eye of wisdom."...What needs to be abandoned is one's perversions and false clingings.... This applies not only to actual life but to words, concepts, understanding, systems of understanding.[188]

EGO AND NON-EGO

In the tantric system, any worldly pleasure, any experience of the senses, any occasion in this world can become an opportunity for enlightenment when wisdom is applied. We have seen that wisdom *(prajna)* implies non-exclusiveness, non-attachment, the principle of relativity, shunyata.

The greatest obstacle is the ego. Ego—or rather one's *view* of one's "I"—is at the root of all problems and sufferings according to Buddhist thought. When Buddhists talk about ego they refer to the illusory belief in a solid, concrete, separate entity, independent and disconnected from any other phenomena. In that sense naturally the ego becomes an insurmountable barrier between oneself and the rest of the world, with no possibility of true communication and communion, not only with others but also with the depth of oneself. That barrier has to be demolished, and that is the chief problem in the path to liberation.

The aim, then, is not so much the dissolution of the ego as it is the dissolution of the false view of the ego; and what is to be achieved is an openness to all possibilities that present themselves, and above all, a realization that we are infinitely more than we believe we are when identified with our concrete little ego. We have limitless potentials, once we are free from the bondage of our ego-centric world: the Buddhist would say, we can become a buddha.

Indeed, according to Jung, the ego, full of distortions and projections, needs to be dissolved before the Self can emerge. The Self, however, which is the totality of the psyche, includes the ego. In the process of individuation one does not destroy the ego, rather one places it in subordinate relation to the Self. The ego is no longer the center of the personality; the Self, the mandala, which unites all opposites, is its center. What is dissolved is the inflated, concrete ego, pursuing its exclusive selfish purposes, just following its own impulses. The individuated ego, in relation to the Self, is not only needed for adequate functioning on what the Buddhists refer to as the mundane level of reality; it is also of crucial importance in the encounter with the transpersonal, in order to preserve the integrity of the psyche.

For Jung, transformation is the goal of psychotherapy, and the disappearance of egohood is the only criterion of change. But he maintains that frequently for Westerners "a conscious ego and a cultivated understanding must first be produced through analysis before one can even think about abolishing egohood."[189]

However, in the alchemical sense of *solutio*, the dissolution of a dry, hard soil of ego-consciousness through a confrontation with and fertilization by the fluid unconscious is a necessary prerequisite for transmutation to take place. This is another way of viewing the sacrifice of the personal ego to the transpersonal Self, the ongoing process of death and rebirth. The experience of nonduality, the mystical experience, or every creative act must go through that process.

The illusion of a permanent, separate ego does not mean there is no individuality. Our essential oneness with the universe, in the view of Lama Govinda,

> ...is not sameness or unqualified identity, but an organic relationship, in which differentiation and uniqueness of function are as important as that ultimate or basic unity.
>
> Individuality and universality are not mutually exclusive values, but two sides of the same reality, compensating, fulfilling, and complementing each other, and becoming one in the experience of enlightenment. This experience does not dissolve the mind into an amorphous All, but rather brings the realization that the individual itself contains the totality focalized in its very core.[190]

Universality and individuality, unity and diversity, pleroma and creatura, nirvana and samsara, the "two sides of the same reality"; there could not be one without its opposite.

SUFFERING AND METHODS OF HEALING

Both Buddhism and Jung have as their primary concern relief of suffering. In fact the whole Buddhist system has evolved around that core idea initially formulated by Buddha in the four noble truths that all life is suffering, but there can be an end to it. In Mahayana Buddhism the ideal of the bodhisattva, the symbol of compassion, is the ultimate expression of the underlying concern to lead every being to freedom from suffering, to enlightenment.

Jung too tells us in his autobiography and throughout his writings that he is concerned with the healing of human suffering. "We do not profess," he says,

> ...a psychology with merely academic pretensions, or seek explanations that have no bearing on life. What we want is a practical psychology which yields approvable results—one which explains things in a way that must be justified by the outcome for the patient.[191]

But unlike Buddha, Jung does not perceive the possibility of an end to suffering. In his view happiness and suffering represent another pair of opposites, indispensable to life, and one cannot exist without the other. He states:

> Man has to cope with the problem of suffering. The Oriental wants to get rid of suffering by casting it off. Western man tries to suppress suffering with drugs. But suffering has to be overcome and the only way to overcome it is to endure it. We learn that only from him [the Crucified Christ].[192]

At another time, Jung discusses the double-edged possibility of the consequences of suffering: it can be a discipline "needed for the emotional chaos of man, though at the same time it can kill the living spirit...it remains forever an unresolved question whether suffering is educative or demoralizing…. Man's fate has always swung between day and night. There is nothing we can do to change this."[193] Thus suffering has the potential of becoming a "psychic mover," a prelude to the process of healing and individuation or it can lead to pathology. The painful symptoms of a neurosis often are the expression of the psyche's urge toward wholeness. The symptoms contain seeds of potentials to be actualized, and when they are worked with rather than avoided or suppressed, they become sources of new achievements, new integration—"the dark night of the soul" turns into illumination. Jung experienced that throughout his life. On the other hand, excessive, overwhelming suffering, particularly in an individual whose inner constitution is weak and the ego disconnected from the Self, can lead to diametrically opposite directions: madness, criminality, and other kinds of pathology.

The path leading via the underworld to illumination, to the Self, is by no means an easy one. It requires the sacrifice of our most-cherished possession, our ego, so that the Self can emerge. Similarly Buddhists say the root of all suffering is attachment to ego, and they urge us to relinquish it, so that our true nature, our buddha nature, can be revealed. But this can only come about spontaneously; it cannot be forced, either with Jung's therapeutic methods or with any Buddhist methods.

In both systems the path differs with each individual, and it is always carried on within individuals as their own unique inner work. Jung's process of individuation, his journey to wholeness, is a very individual pursuit. Jung was even opposed to the use of groups as a psychotherapeutic method. The path of the Buddhist adept is likewise very individual, although it makes use of group practice, recognizing the powerful energy that is generated from it, and especially from participation in rituals.

It is invariably, in both systems, a nondogmatic, empirical method aimed at the living inner experience, a dynamic way of going inward, where we can discover the seed of enlightenment, the Self, within in each of us. "No textbook can teach psychology;

one learns by actual experience"[194]—says Jung. And in another passage he writes: "In psychology one possesses nothing unless one has experienced it in reality. Hence a purely intellectual insight is not enough, because one knows only the words and not the substance of the thing from inside."[195]

The cognitive function, though, is not minimized in Jung or in Buddhism. According to the Tibetans, "Intellectual understanding increases the power of the rational mind and this increases the power of formal meditation."[196] After listening to the teaching, disciples must try to understand it through reason before they can transform it into living reality. And then if it does not correspond to their experience of living reality they should abandon it. Is that not what Jung tells us when he maintains that a conscious understanding must precede the disappearance of egohood? And furthermore, is he not in his psychology primarily concerned with practical results that must be justified by the subjective experience of the patient he is treating?

The first noble truth, which is that the nature of life is suffering, must first be clearly understood before anything else can be done. It has been said that the path leading to liberation is completed through intellectual as well as moral and spiritual perfection. In the Buddhist practice of mindfulness one is closely attentive to the activities of the mind, ideas and thoughts, sensations and feelings. And in tantra especially, all the hidden tendencies, projections, must be known and experienced before they can be transmuted into wisdom.

In Jungian analysis one must deal with one's shadow, the dark rejected part of the psyche; one must detect projections and egocentric aims. The intensity of the emotional turmoil is not repressed or devalued, but the energy that is contained there is utilized in the process of change. Similarly in tantric practices the energy of the emotions, like anger, desire, aversion, etc., is mobilized to transmute the passion. Both systems fully recognize the potential destructiveness of hidden unconscious tendencies. For that reason the total psyche must be approached, its dark as well

as its light aspects, personified in tantra by peaceful and wrathful deities repeatedly constructed and dissolved in one's visualization. One is continually facing the conflict of opposites in the
effort to transcend them. This is the purpose of the *sadhanas*
(meditation exercises), which are based on a profound understanding of what Jung would call depth psychology.

In Jungian analysis, the transcendent function is the comparable principle that is aimed at in the dialectic process between
analysts and analysands. The latter on their way to individuation are reconciling the conflicting parts of their psyche, the split
between the conscious ego and the unconscious and reaching
beyond all pairs of opposites.

In both systems the yogi, or the analysand, must eventually
become independent of outside support. The methods used in
working on inner growth vary infinitely, depending on the person, the time, and the circumstances. Buddha used a different
language to teach the same truth to different people, being aware
of the importance of individual characteristics and needs. "Since
individuality...is absolutely unique, unpredictable, and uninter-
pretable," Jung stresses, "the therapist must abandon all his preconceptions and techniques."[197] The integrity of the psyche of the
other is highly respected and never to be violated by imposing
one's own definitions and preconceived ideas. In this manner true
communication can be established. This is Jung's view, but it is
also in the spirit of the Madhyamaka philosophy.

Transformation comes about through the vehicle of symbols.
Jung recognized that "any imagination is a potentiality,"[198] and
through his method of active imagination found a way of healing and transforming the personality. Similarly in tantric meditation the initiate becomes impregnated with the symbols
visualized, the deities—all different symbols of Buddha—and is
transformed into a buddha.

In the tantric model Jung discerned an analogy to his
psychology of the unconscious. He points out that tantra deals
with contents that are "constantly reproduced by our uncon-

scious in this form or another.... This is not mysticism, this is psychology."[199]

Note should be made of the powerful symbology that Tibetan Buddhists use in their iconography, their sacred texts, and their rituals, all designed to express the inexpressible and to evoke certain experiences that transport the individual to higher levels of consciousness beyond mundane reality. The teachings are done in a style that is poetic, imaginal, and often repetitive. In his writings Jung also makes abundant use of repetition, circumambulation, and paradoxes, and avoids a language and style that is purely rational. He tells us that

> in describing the living process of the psyche, I deliberately and consciously give preference to a dramatic, mythological way of thinking and speaking, because this is not only more expressive but also more exact than an abstract scientific terminology.[200]

REDEMPTION OF GOD

The idea of psychic transformation is fundamental to tantra, Jung, and alchemy. In tantra adepts identify with the divine qualities, and through this process, they become aware of their own divine essence. The Buddhist, we are told,

> believes in the divine principle in man, the inborn spark of light *(bodhicitta)* embodied in his consciousness as a yearning toward perfection, toward completeness, toward Enlightenment. To put it paradoxically, it is not God who creates man, but man who creates God in his image, i.e., the idea of the divine aim within himself, which he realizes in the fires of suffering from which compassion, understanding, love and wisdom are born.
>
> The unfoldment of individual life in the universe has no other aim apparently but to become conscious of its

own divine essence, and since this process goes on continuously, it represents a perpetual birth of God or, to put it into Buddhist terminology, the continuous arising of Enlightened Beings, in each of whom the totality of the universe becomes conscious.[201]

Here we find an extraordinary parallel to Jung's thought that "the creator...needs Man to illuminate his creation."[202] and that this work can be accomplished only in the individual psyche, which is the carrier of the divine spark.

Let us listen to Jung speaking on this subject:

Although the divine incarnation is a cosmic and absolute event, it only manifests empirically in those relatively few individuals capable of enough consciousness to make ethical decisions, i.e., to decide for the Good. Therefore God can be called good only in as much as He is able to manifest His goodness in individuals. His moral quality depends upon individuals. That is why He incarnates. Individuation and individual existence are indispensable for the transformation of God the Creator.[203]

The Mahayana bodhisattva has attained the highest state of consciousness and through his actions and attitudes, his wisdom and compassion, is, in Jung's terms, an active force in furthering "the transformation of God." He is, it seems to me, the most fully accomplished individuated person on whom God depends to illuminate his creation. Both Jung and Buddhists affirm that only human beings can perform that task in the universe—therefore the necessity for human existence, or as Tibetan Buddhists would say, for "the precious human rebirth." This is perhaps the true meaning of the Mahayana ideal of the bodhisattva whose sole and unique purpose in this world is to work for the benefit of all beings. And when bodhisattvas are teaching and inspiring those on the path to liberation continuously and progressively to expand their consciousness, they are leading them toward those inward experiences intimated by Jung and alluded to in his statement that: "...it can be expected that we are going to contact spheres of a not yet transformed God when our consciousness begins to extend into the sphere of the unconscious."[204]

However, the difference between the Mahayana Buddhist and Jung is that in Jung's thought the unconscious can never be totally conscious and the process of individuation is never completed, whereas to the Buddhist it is possible to know all of the unknowable and become fully enlightened. We should be reminded here that in his entire work, Jung is only considering psychological experiences that can be established empirically and is not dealing with metaphysical categories. Therefore, Jung states,

> ...when God or the Tao is named an impulse of the soul, or a psychic state, something has been said about the knowable only, but nothing about the unknowable, about which nothing can be determined.[205]

In Jung's view, although it is man's task to reach maximum levels of consciousness, any increase of it brings an additional burden. This is diametrically opposed to the view of Mahayana Buddhists that consciousness is at the source of liberation, and it is bliss. The actual process in reaching the goal is by no means free from tortures. The advanced disciple may be put to all kinds of tests, and the experiences endured are not unlike the frightful and tormenting visions of the alchemist Zosimos.[206] But the end result is nothing short of bliss. Bliss is consistently emphasized in tantric meditation, and it is an experience that comes even to the less-advanced meditator. The cheerfulness and infectious laughter of Tibetan lamas, their exuberance coupled with calm and peacefulness, their exquisite spontaneity, warmth, and openness reflect the state of mind of human beings unencumbered by problems and burdens of daily life, material or psychological, nor by fear of death. This is the very first impression invariably gained by anyone who has had the good fortune and privilege to meet them. By their attitude and behavior it is as though they want to convey to us, in a wordless but clear, unequivocal language, that it is indeed possible to transcend suffering, as their first master had taught them.

In contrast, Jung does not propose to help his patients end their suffering. He believes that: "Life demands for its completion and fulfillment a balance between joy and sorrow."[207] While he contends that suffering is a natural, not unhealthy aspect of life, and happiness an impossible state to attain, Tibetan Buddhists claim that suffering can be transmuted into happiness.

However, Buddhists, as well as Jung, and the alchemists, perceive that the major task to accomplish is the redemption of the divine spark within. To the tantric Buddhist it means finding the deity hidden in the unconscious and suffocated by the ego. To Jung it is the conscious realization of the Self, and its separation from the ego. To the alchemist it is the redemption of the *anima mundi* imprisoned in matter.

JUNG'S VIEW OF EASTERN TRADITIONS

One can find many paradoxes and inconsistencies in Jung's writings, and his views of Eastern traditions are a good example of this. At times Jung is speaking in favor of Eastern traditions, praising their ways of approaching the psyche and their intuitive wisdom, which the West lacks, and at other times he warns Westerners against the dangers of embracing a system that is foreign to their culture.

Personally I am amazed at Jung's penetrating understanding (despite occasional misconceptions) of the Eastern systems, including the Tibetan tradition, without having had the benefit of direct contact with the latter and without experiencing their meditative practices. I am just as amazed today at some of the Tibetan lamas' keen perceptiveness and sensitivity to the West and its lifestyle. I have often pondered over it, and I suggest that in both cases this is due to the intuitive wisdom of a clear, unprejudiced mind that is capable of transcending historical and cultural barriers and reaching valid conclusions.

Jung sees vast differences between the Eastern and Western standpoints and raises the question of the possibility and advisability of their imitating each other.[208] Along with this, he also tells us that in the human psyche the collective unconscious "possesses a common substratum transcending all differences in culture and consciousness."[209] This unconscious psyche, by virtue of being common to all human beings, contains "latent predispositions toward identical reactions."[210] Indeed, Jung is aware of the close parallels between Eastern and Western psychology.[211] His concern, though, is that Westerners will adopt Eastern values from their usual extroverted position, and make dogmas out of them, rather than seek those values within themselves, within their own psyche. He finds that the core of Eastern teachings consists in inward looking of the mind, which in itself has a self-liberating power. He is very critical of the Westerners who merely attempt to imitate and whose endeavors remain superficial and therefore useless and, more than that, even damaging to their psyche. Jung remarks:

> One cannot be too cautious in these matters, for what with the imitative urge and a positively morbid avidity to possess themselves of outlandish feathers and deck themselves out in this exotic plumage, far too many people are misled into snatching at such "magical" ideas and applying them externally, like an ointment. People will do anything, no matter how absurd, in order to avoid facing their own Souls.[212]

Jung says that the basic problem, whether in the Eastern or Western world, "is not so much a withdrawal from the objects of desire, as a more detached attitude to desire as such, no matter what its object."[213] In this respect he fully understood one of the principal postulates of tantra, that it is not desire as such, but lack of control, possessiveness, and attachment to desire that brings about a confused state of mind, and consequently suffering. Hence the need to see all phenomena as impermanent and empty.

Jung cannot conceive of the possibility of achieving total nonduality, a state of at-onement. "One cannot know something that is not distinct from oneself.... I therefore assume that, in this point, Eastern intuition has overreached itself."[214] In making this statement Jung seems to forget that his own concepts are often irrational and paradoxical, and besides that, nonduality on a transpersonal level does not exclude individuality on a conventional level of existence. Furthermore, experiences of nonduality are not unknown in the Western tradition either. I am referring here to the disciplines and contemplative exercises of medieval monastic life, when the individual for a moment felt in unity with God, or rather *was* God,[215] like the tantric meditator who becomes the deity he visualizes.

In many ways Jung comes closer to Eastern systems than to Western traditions despite his insistence that Westerners should stay with their own traditions, their symbols and mythology. Along with the Buddhists, he rejects dogmas, and in his psychology, as in Buddhist teaching, it is only the subjective, inner experience that validates the theory. Jung himself had profound inner experiences, and it is from the depth of his soul that he gained direct immediate knowledge, which he then translated into his work. In that respect he was following the gnostic tradition. The latter had inspired and influenced him before Eastern traditions came to his attention. Scholars have suggested that Hindu or Buddhist traditions influenced gnosticism, although there is no conclusive evidence.[216] It may be that the human mind independently produced similar or identical ideas in two different parts of the world. This would only confirm Jung's concept of the common structure of the psyche, transcending cultural differences. But whatever its origin, gnosticism has more than superficial parallels with Buddhism.

In comparing these two systems one finds many analogies. Some of the most salient of these include the idea of human liberation through internal transformation; of the psyche carrying within itself the potential for liberation; the emphasis on the primacy of immediate experience; and the need for initial guidance but the eventual freedom from any external authority. Both systems also see the disciples' own minds as their guide, and that it is there that they must discover the truth. A further similarity is the belief that not sin but ignorance, lack of self-knowledge, is the source of suffering and enslavement by unconscious impulses: the one who remains ignorant lives in illusion and cannot experience fulfillment. And, of course, the discovery of the divine within is central to each: the one who achieves gnosis is no longer a Christian but becomes Christ.[217]

Here a passage from the Gnostic Gospel of Philip is remarkable in its similarity to the fundamental tantric view:

> ...You saw the spirit, you became spirit. You saw Christ, you became Christ. You saw [the Father, you] shall become Father...you see yourself, and *what you see you shall [become]*.[218]

And now another passage implying that the Kingdom of God is but the symbol for a transformed state of consciousness:

> Jesus said..."When you make the two one, and when you make the inside like the outside and the outside like the inside, and the above like the below, and when you make the male and the female one and the same...then you will enter [the Kingdom]."[219]

It appears obvious that Buddhist and Gnostic Christian symbols express the same inner experiences, and, whether the disciple adopts one or the other, the essential quest for meaning and spatial and temporal transcendence is the same. Therefore when

Jung penetrated the depth of his psyche and thereby gained access to direct knowledge arising out of his own transformative experience, he became a link in the chain of ancient mystical traditions, Buddhist and Christian. Or to put it differently, in the depth of the collective unconscious—or the height of his supraconsciousness—Jung met the consciousness of the medieval Christian mystics, like Meister Eckhart, and that of the tantric masters. The words expressing the ineffable experience, the union with the Buddha Mind, or with God (which is beyond words anyway), and the tools used in the process may differ, but the core of the experience does not: in the heart of it, for the briefest moment, the gap between various traditions is closed. And it is precisely there that I am looking for parallels between Jungian and tantric systems. The methods and techniques that Jung developed in the context of, and to conform with, the Western tradition and mythological images, and with the sociocultural conditions of contemporary Europe and America, are less important. They reflect only the necessity to remain rooted in one's own culture, which Jung recognized, and which Tibetan Buddhists would acknowledge too. And most of all, every Buddhist would be in perfect agreement with Jung's statement that "We must get at the Eastern values from within and not from without, seeking them in ourselves."[220]

DANGERS

Both Jung and tantric Buddhists are aware of the latent risks inherent in the practice of their respective methods. Jung repeatedly warns us of the possible dangerous effects when releasing unconscious contents without proper safeguards and precautions, as it may overwhelm consciousness and cause its collapse, resulting in serious consequences, even psychosis. He compares the potential explosive power of the archetypes to that of the released atom, and he says:

> The archetypes have this peculiarity in common with the
> atomic world, which is...that the more deeply the inves-
> tigator penetrates into the universe of microphysics the
> more devastating are the explosive forces he finds
> enchained there.[221]

For this reason, as already noted, it is of crucial importance to have a strong, well-developed psychic structure before confronting the unconscious; in this way mental equilibrium can be maintained.

Tantric masters issue very similar warnings, namely, that the methods they teach are profound but also extremely powerful and therefore hazardous unless the proper preparations are made, and the disciple is led into the practice gradually under the guidance of a qualified teacher. They furthermore stress the importance of relating at all times to the actuality of one's experience, to the solid, earthy aspect of it.[222] This is where Jung would agree: he knew so well how crucial it was for him to keep on with his daily work, maintain close contact with his family, and fulfill his other obligations while in the midst of his own confrontation with the unconscious.

Tibetan Buddhists urge Westerners not to abandon the values of their own culture. In fact a proper understanding of one's own culture and being deeply rooted in it—they would say—is a prerequisite for venturing into and benefiting from practices of a foreign tradition. There is also always the danger of grasping the literal rather than the intrinsic meaning of symbols and rituals, and thereby going astray and getting lost in one's practice.

Tantric images visualized in meditation represent archetypes, and therefore, particular caution is needed in dealing with them. As every archetype has a double aspect—a light and a dark one—the power of its dark side when it suddenly emerges from the depth of the unconscious may cause delusional fantasies and loss of touch with reality. For example, the archetype of the Great Mother contains such paradoxical aspects as nurturing and creating, as well as devouring and destroying. A fragile individual whose conscious-

ness is not well developed may become disoriented by the emergence of the archetype in its unexpected terrifying aspect.[223] I have
been a witness to this unfortunate effect on Western students, on
more than one occasion, at intensive meditation courses.

ETHICAL ISSUES

Atisha, the eleventh-century Indian sage responsible for a revival
of Buddhism in Tibet, said: "When the container and its contents
are filled with wrongs, change this adverse circumstance into the
path to full awakening."[224] This admonition could just as well be
made to the people of the twenty-first century. Tibetans today
recognize that since we are living in an age of degeneration when
both the environment—the container—and its inhabitants—the
contents—are polluted and afflicted with enormous and dangerous problems, this is especially the time to use the prevailing situation as an encouragement to cultivate our minds, transform
our outlook, or as they say, to change the adverse circumstances
into the path to liberation.[225]

Jung on the other hand was also extremely concerned, in this
time of confusion, with the fate of our civilization and the danger of humanity destroying itself. He discerned, however, that

> We are living in what the Greeks called *Kairos*—the right
> time—for a "metamorphosis of the gods"...So much is at
> stake and so much depends on the psychological consti-
> tution of modern man.[226]

According to Jung—and this is the same idea that Tibetan
Buddhists are proposing—the change must begin with individuals, in their own psyche, their greatest instrument. To Jung that
implies self-knowledge, knowing the dark side of the psyche, the
unconscious as well as its conscious aspects, and reconciling the
polarities. Without this knowledge, unconscious contents cause
projections and illusions that falsify our relations with others,

and that is where the wars begin. "Right action comes from right thinking, and…there is no cure and no improving of the world that does not begin with the individual himself,"[227] says Jung. The right action and right thinking, is that not what Buddha taught 2,500 years ago?

The more conscious we become of our unconscious drives and act accordingly, the less contaminated with projections are our relations with the world, and the more open we are to enter into communication, yes, even communion with it. Jung talks of society's need for an affective bond, the principle of *caritas,* the Christian love of the neighbor. He warns us that: "Where love stops, power begins, and violence, and terror."[228]

Compassion is the basic element in Buddhist philosophy and psychology, and in Tibetan Buddhism it is inseparable from wisdom, the enlightened state of mind. Today the Dalai Lama, who is regarded as the incarnation of Avalokiteshvara, the buddha of compassion, is teaching and bringing to the Western world, wherever he goes, the ideal of kindness and compassion as a means to achieve harmony in the world on the principle of universal responsibility.

The Buddhist concept of emptiness is sometimes misinterpreted in the West as implying annulment of ethical considerations. Jung suspected that Westerners' attempt at detachment as a way of liberation, which they learned from yogic practices, was only a way of liberation from moral responsibilities.[229]

Buddhism is one of the most highly developed ethical as well as psychological systems. Ethical issues and individual responsibility are always and without exception an integral part of its philosophy and practice. The rule applies to all schools and of course to tantric Buddhism as well.

And Jung, a psychologist and physician, in all his multidimensional work, and his entire life, consistently reminded us as humans of our unique responsibility and ethical obligation to transform ourselves, or shall I say, to transform God.

6 Conclusion

In drawing to a close, I should like to make a few points to high-light the conclusions reached in my attempt to understand and find possible parallels between Buddhism and Jung's psychology.

The two systems were born and developed in areas widely apart from each other, geographically, historically, and cultur-ally, and were separated in time by a span of two and a half mil-lennia. Yet both, despite all the differences, are concerned with the same human problems, and have found that solutions are to be sought, uniquely, within the psyche of each individual.

The overriding concern of Buddhism is termination of suf-fering. Jung's major task was the healing of man's psychic wounds. However, the Buddhist believes that total deliverance from suffering is possible; Jung's view is that suffering is in the nature of life and is even a necessary ingredient that can never be completely eliminated.

The ultimate goal in both systems is for us to become what we truly are. For the Mahayana Buddhist that means to achieve buddhahood; every being without exception has that potential. For Jung it means to achieve wholeness, realize one's Self, which is an urge inherent in the psyche. The path to buddhahood is extremely long, but it is believed that by practicing tantric meth-ods it can be reached within a single lifetime. For Jung, though, self-realization is a never-ending process.

Progressive development of consciousness through intro-spection is the initial goal of both Buddhism and Jung's psychol-ogy. But the Buddhist maintains that consciousness can be developed fully so that no unconscious content can disturb the mind, and consequently perfect control can be achieved—the state of pure awareness. Consciousness to the Buddhist is associated with bliss: knowing is happiness, unknowing is suffering. Jung does not believe that pure consciousness, uncontaminated by the unconscious, can ever be attained. Furthermore, integration of the unconscious into consciousness, the reconciliation of opposites, entails not elimination of the unconscious, or the control of it, but a concession to both aspects of the psyche.

The principle and use of opposites is fundamental in Jung's model, as it is in Buddhism, and is particularly emphasized in tantric practices.

Both systems require that every aspect of the individual be involved in the process; nothing is to be rejected. Knowledge and intellectual understanding are important, especially in the initial stages of the path, but they have to be complemented by feeling and intuition, and the insight gained in the course of contemplation or meditation has to be translated into action and become a moral duty.

The path starts and ends in the psyche, the mind. Jung claims he does not make philosophical or metaphysical statements and that his work is based on empirical evidence only. Buddhism by contrast, being a religion, necessarily deals with philosophical and metaphysical categories. However, Buddha himself refused to answer questions pertaining to the nature of the Absolute, knowing that philosophical arguments create discord and confusion and do not add to the solution of suffering, the primary problem. He taught instead the middle way, later to be elaborated by the Madhyamaka school, whose basic attitude is freedom from dogmatism and the dialectical approach, attempting to resolve theoretical conflicts by rising to a higher standpoint.

This in a way is Jung's approach to his own work and practice. There are no definitive theories or therapeutic methods applicable indiscriminately to everyone, since every individual is unique in his or her specific situation. At the same time, in assisting the person through his conflicts, and on his journey to individuation, Jung would apply the method of first bringing to consciousness and objectively observing the facts of his inner and outer life; then, by use of the imagination, amplifying them and raising the conflict and dilemma to a higher level of consciousness, leading from the personal to the transpersonal—the approach to the numinous.

In both tantra and Jung's system, symbols are abundantly made use of as vehicles and means to transform our awareness and our ordinary reality into a significant one. In tantric Buddhism symbolic images and visualization practices are specifically defined by tradition, although there is latitude given to the meditator, and generally creative imagination is encouraged and fostered. Jung's model, having much less of a tradition, allows a purely individual, unstructured way of exercising one's imagination in the service of developing self-knowledge. Both ways lead to the Self—the center, or heart, of the mandala.

Buddhist teachings and Jung's therapeutic methods are invariably adapted to the specific needs, conditions, and capacities of the individual; the guru and the therapist are guides on the way. They are never regarded as ultimate authorities: the psyche or mind of the individual—the only instrument through which one experiences reality—is the sole authority. In Buddhism one is constantly urged to test with one's experience the validity of the teaching, and adopt or reject it in accordance with one's own findings. Similarly Jung has enormous respect for the integrity of the psyche and a trust in its capacity to function objectively— when not interfered with—and thus to lead the individual toward his true destination, his Self.

Both systems warn against dangers and urge the initiate to take necessary precautions and safeguards when contacting powerful inner forces, potentially disruptive to the psychic structure of the personality. For this reason Tibetan Buddhism, especially in its tantric form, has traditionally observed a measure of secrecy.

In both systems passions, emotions, positive or negative, are not suppressed but transformed in the mind by utilizing the very energy they contain.

Contradictions, paradoxes, and imaginal language abound in Jung's work and in Buddhism in general, and tantric Buddhism in particular, but neither Jung nor Buddhists are concerned about that. They are regarded as means of portraying the fullness and richness of life and different ways of perceiving it, which conventional language with its limitations is unable to express.

Tantra's chief concern is spiritual growth, and the remarkable tantric way is one not of asceticism but of fully experiencing life in all its joy, spontaneity, and creativity. An essential part of it, however, is the mental attitude, that is, the selfless motivation that underscores every form of Buddhist practice. In tantra and in Jung's model the mundane and spiritual dimensions of life are closely connected; in fact they are two sides of the same reality that need to be reconciled.

In Jung's work, the element of compassion, the principle of Eros, is not emphasized as it is in Tibetan Buddhism, although he too is keenly concerned with the fate of humanity, and above all that of the inner man. As a psychologist and physician he knows that we can heal ourselves only by relinquishing ego-centered pursuits and connecting ourselves to a larger context of life. In the process of it, in our depths, on the archetypal level where there is no separation, we become related to the rest of humanity, and compassion spontaneously arises. Nevertheless, Jung's psychology naturally has a less-encompassing scope than Buddhism, a psychological and ethical system that has a religious basis.

Yet it has become obvious to me that Tibetan Buddhists and C. G. Jung—and the alchemists—each coming from their own unique directions, are pointing out to us, by means of their own unique words and symbols, a wisdom that is universal. It has been said that the West has a wealth of its own symbols and that there is no need to seek others in the East. Indeed it would be a pity and a great loss to reject the rich Western symbolism. Yet Eastern symbols are fresh to the Western mind and therefore possess a greater capacity to inspire and stimulate the imagination, while unfortunately for many in the West our symbols have become ossified and thus have lost their intrinsic meaning. The stirrings of the soul can come from many different sources; does it really matter which is the one? If it is true that the ultimate wisdom is one and the same, whether discovered in one's buddha nature, the Self, or the Philosopher's Stone, we should be able to find in seemingly remote and esoteric traditions values that speak to us in a language that is relevant to the Western world. Perhaps Jung's model will be preferable to some Westerners, as certain of its forms and aspects may be more easily adapted to their needs and lifestyle. Some, on the other hand, will find a greater affinity to the Tibetan model. And some others still, will perceive no contradiction between the two and will be immeasurably enriched by the treasures they both so generously offer.

The appearance of the Tibetans in the West must be more than the result of a historical turn of events that began in a tragedy. I perceive in it another tangible manifestation of the law of opposites: the abysmal deterioration of moral and spiritual values in our materialistic and militaristic civilization had to produce its counterbalance, the arrival of the holy beings from Tibet, who descended from the top of the world into the valleys of the Western hemisphere. As Jung already sensed and pointed out to us, there is much to learn from the East. Tibetan lamas with their profound wisdom and compassionate hearts, their serene manners and gentle speech, have much to teach us. And especially in their silent meditations, they speak to us, each one of us individually, in a direct and forceful way. But most of all, they are living symbols of enlightened beings—of the highest aspirations and attainment of which humans are capable. It is the lamas' very presence among us that is the unique and most significant contribution of the Tibetan tradition to the Western world.

When the roaring, giant iron birds flew and brought the Tibetans into our midst, it marked not only the fulfillment of an age-old prophecy: it was a synchronistic moment in which the worlds of spirit and matter came together. Birds, symbols of freedom, in their iron form became the vehicles of some extraordinary human beings who, in their minds and hearts, are carriers of true spiritual freedom in its living actualized form. So, the iron birds have joined their spiritual counterparts.

CODA

It is extremely difficult to understand tantric Buddhism, and it is even more difficult to write about it, since its foundation lies not in knowledge but in individual experience. The same is true of Jung's work. Thus I am painfully aware of the inadequacy, and the omissions and inevitable distortions that a book like this must contain.

From the outset I have been also well aware that the task I have given myself is tremendously ambitious, considering the limitless proportions of the subject matter. But it is even much more than that: the task is awesome. There is no possibility of encompassing both disciplines, of conveying their numinous, their dynamic, flowing, and ever-changing aspects, which is how I have experienced the essence both of Jung's *opus* and of Tibetan Buddhism.

With this in mind, for a long time I could not start writing. I could see the image of the future work in my inner vision, but I could not put it into words. Then I had a dream in which a voice gently whispered to me: "The Self and Padma." The Self and Padma, the Western and Eastern symbols of spiritual unfoldment and totality—this was what my book-to-be was all about. What else needed to be said: it was all there, told in four brief words. But this was only the beginning. And the dream was a signal that I could now start writing. Shortly afterward I embarked on the journey. Indeed it was like a journey, long, hard, and tortuous, with some moments of near despair, alternating with those of exhilaration. I soon realized that the act of writing and building this book was like a meditative process. It was like an alchemical *opus* too, starting with the *massa confusa,* and leading up through the various stages to final crystallization into its essence. And along the way, as the work was building, its inner meaning was gradually unfolding to me.

After I had gone around and around a long, tedious road, intermittently getting lost and finding my way back, slowly, and painfully or joyously circumambulating, I came to the same point I started from, but this time the message was imprinted deeply into my mind and soul:

the Self and Padma.

Epilogue

My religion is very simple. My religion is kindness.
—His Holiness the Fourteenth Dalai Lama

The world hangs on a thin thread,
and that is the psyche of man.
—C. G. Jung

Since wars begin in the minds of men, it is in the minds of
men that the defenses of peace must be constructed.
—Preamble to UNESCO's Constitution

Jung made a quantum leap in psychology. Whatever one writes about Jung can only be a pale attempt to describe the magnitude of his work, which goes far beyond the fields of psychiatry and psychology: his discoveries had a major impact on art and literature, science, ecology, theology, and on the understanding of the importance of religion in our lives. Much of his work is visionary, prophetic, and eminently relevant to the present world situation. Jung's psychology is a work of art, not only because some of his writings are beautifully poetic, but above all because he is capable of inspiring us individually in different ways and transforming our consciousness, just as any great art does. Moreover, each time we read Jung we are surprised with new discoveries; something hidden is revealed to us as we grow, deepen our understanding, and touch more subtle levels of consciousness. This, too, is a hallmark of great works of art.

As one approaches Jung's work and some of his original ideas concerning the collective unconscious, alchemy and psychotherapy, the meaning of the mandala, and the Self—all depicting the process of individuation— one discovers unknown places in oneself, makes new connections, and reaches fresh insights. But one must tread slowly and gradually lest one remain on the surface and gain merely a shallow intellectual comprehension. Jung repeatedly reminds us that only direct experience has real value.

All that can be said of encountering Jung's work applies equally to the teachings of Tibetan Buddhism. Both traditions tell us that one must be quiet and silent, the mind cleansed from outer and inner pollution, and allow the unconscious to speak while we listen to our inner wisdom, which is our true guru.

The nature and the workings of the mind are basic topics in Buddhist teachings, just as mind/psyche is in Jung's work. Understanding the mind is closely related to understanding the experience of suffering. Tibetan Buddhism discusses at length the various aspects of inevitable human suffering, from which no one is immune, but we in the West prefer to ignore it, stressing instead a narrow understanding of our cherished "pursuit of happiness." Despite this pursuit, millions suffer from depression, alcoholism, and other addictions; suicide and violence are widespread among people of all ages and walks of life. There exists a plethora of "afflictive emotions," as Buddhists refer to them, or "afflictions of the soul," as Jung calls such inner psychic conflicts. Individuals whose lives are fragmented and meaningless are far from free to pursue happiness; they can only seek to escape from suffering, loneliness, and despair through whatever destructive means they have at their disposal. Tragically, they become the breeding ground of anger, hatred, and violence toward themselves and others.

We learn from Jung that psychological health requires a meaningful life. The quest for meaning is the innate and spontaneous urge to self-realization and wholeness or completeness, to become true to one's inner nature; this is the task of individuation, the path to the heart—to freedom. The urge toward self-realization, as aspiration to buddhahood, is also the central concept of Buddhist psychology. It is the urge of the mind to awaken, to become conscious, which is what the word *buddha* means: awakened one. Jung points out that the task of individuation—which involves paying serious attention to the unconscious as well as the conscious contents of our psyche—is imposed on us by nature.

> If...[man] does this consciously and intentionally, he avoids all the unhappy consequences of repressed individuation. In other words, if he voluntarily takes the burden of completeness on himself he need not find it "happening" to him against his will in a negative form. [230]

Or, as Jesus preaches in the Gospel of Thomas: "If you bring forth what is within you, what you bring forth will save you. If you do not bring forth what is within you, what you do not bring forth will destroy you." In *The Tibetan Book of the Dead* we encounter an analogous message: one must work with one's unconscious material during life to avoid a terrifying transition to the afterlife.

Inherent in the concept of individuation is the archetype of the Self, which is the principle of meaning and the culmination of psychic growth. The Self is the totality of the psyche—conscious and unconscious—whereas the ego is the center of consciousness with its personal contents only. In the process of individuation, as the Self develops, the ego assumes a subordinate position; there is a shift from the purely personal ego as the center of personality to the transpersonal Self. The Self is the symbol of man's divinity, or the God within, the buddha nature, and—like the vajra, a Tibetan Buddhist symbol—it is indestructible. In its pictorial expression it is represented by the mandala, a mystic circle with a nucleus uniting all opposites. As we can see, then, at the heart of Jung's teaching and his psychotherapy is the notion that, after a functional ego has been firmly established, the goal is transformation, the only criterion of which is the disappearance of egohood. This leads to the experience of the Self, the buddha nature, God or Godhead, Christ consciousness, Brahma, the Beloved, Suchness, Tao, Truth, Wholeness—whatever we want to call the mystery that can be experienced but not grasped. But to achieve this transformation one must remain loyal to the law of one's own being; to the extent that we betray that law, we fail to realize life's meaning, and neurosis and alienation ensue along with a variety of mental and emotional imbalances. On the other hand, by constantly following the way of natural development we arrive, in Jung's words, at the experience of the Self, and at the state of being simply what we are. Similarly, in the words of a contemporary Tibetan Buddhist, "The essence of Buddhism is not trying to find something one doesn't have, but recover[ing] what one does have, but doesn't know [one has]."

This is neither an easy task nor a popular undertaking; in fact, it is a perilous adventure, for it runs against convention and collective thinking. Conventions and collective thinking are some of the many obstacles in our world that interfere with the development of our wholeness as individuals. They are powerful, often subtle but brutal. Jung speaks about the individual becoming "a thief and robber to himself....Infected with the leprosy of collective thinking....Our time contains and produces more than enough of that...'arsenical malignity' which prevents man from discovering his true self,"[231] while only what is really oneself has the power to heal. This psychological conflict, I submit, is one of the great dangers in our world, leading to violence and war. When one has become truly oneself, that unique individual—unlike anyone else who has ever lived, an unrepeatable spark in the universe—one no longer has the need for competition, for hatred and hostility, for power to dominate others; compassionate wisdom spontaneously arises. That is why Jung urges us above all to be ourselves, not Jungians, which is very much in the spirit of Buddhism: we must each find our buddha nature in our own unique way. This follows also the old precept of the Greek poet Pindar—a contemporary of Shakyamuni Buddha—namely, "Become what thou art." Or, as Shakespeare says, "To thine own self be true."

Following the path of Buddha and his four noble truths, Tibetan Buddhists teach us how to train and discipline our minds, apply antidotes to counteract our "afflictive emotions," and basically develop our consciousness to deliver ourselves from suffering. However, for Jung "there can be no happiness unless there is suffering...the two cannot exist without each other. So much so that happiness easily turns into suffering even as the most intense suffering can produce a sort of superhuman happiness. They are a pair of opposites that are indispensable to life."[232] He also articulates his view that "suffering has to be overcome, and the only way to overcome it is to endure it."[233] But he believes that "suffering that is not understood is hard to bear, while on the other hand it is often astounding to see how much a person can endure—when he understands the why and wherefore."[234]

The goal of synthesis or reconciliation of opposites in Jung's work, and in Tibetan Buddhism, especially in its tantric form, is of fundamental importance. And in today's divided world it is extremely urgent to reconcile polarities, to hear the other person's, other nations', points of view. But to begin with we need to listen to the argument of our own unconscious, as our conscious, purely rational point of view becomes dangerously rigid, one-sided, and arrogant.

Tibetan Buddhism teaches that our mind/psyche in its true nature is pure and clear. And tantra with its methods, meditation practices, and rituals can lead to the experience of integration of the opposites, of nonduality, or of unity between ourselves and the universe in its totality.[235] It takes place when our desires and all the forces within us, dark and light, have been reconciled and we undergo a transformation: one's Self is elevated to another dimension of reality.

We meet a remarkable parallel to this notion in Jung. In many different ways Jung's voluminous work, culminating in his crowning *opus, Mysterium Coniunctionis,* explores the play of opposites and arrives at the same conclusion. His view of the nature of the psyche is that it is a self-regulatory system that tends to integrate all the opposites in itself—the mystery of the conjunction. And the psyche's transcendental purpose is to experience unity with the *unus mundus,* the one world, or the identity of the personal with the universal Self: in other words, nonduality, the harmony of the universe, experienced by an individual in deep meditation. That is the total freedom and ultimate bliss, the goal of tantra, and I suggest that Jung's entire work gradually leads to that same goal: the experience of *unus mundus.*

The most prominent symbol of opposites in tantra and Jung is the male/female union, exquisitely represented in tantric iconography, and discussed by Jung throughout his work, reflecting the influence of alchemy. This is another significant point where the two systems intersect: the notion of the male and female principles and the meaning of their union. It is most clearly and succinctly expressed by Jung in a commemorative address to his friend, Richard Wilhelm, the sinologist and translator of ancient Chinese texts, who introduced Jung to the world of Chinese alchemy, validating his central idea of the Self, the goal of psychological development.

Here is Jung speaking about Richard Wilhelm, but in many ways it is a portrait of Jung himself:

> As a rule the specialist's is a purely masculine mind, an intellect to which fecundity is an alien and unnatural process, it is therefore an especially ill-adapted tool for giving rebirth to a foreign spirit. But a larger mind bears the stamp of the feminine; it is endowed with a receptive and fruitful womb, which can reshape and give it a familiar form. Wilhelm possessed the rare gift of a maternal intellect. To it he owed his unequalled ability to feel his

way into the spirit of the East and to make his incomparable translations.[236]

I take these moving words to be not only a tribute to a cherished friend, whose work was of an immense importance to Jung, but at the same time a beautiful tribute to the feminine in both women and men, and an expression of respect and deep gratitude to the East for its priceless and enduring contribution to the Western world.

Earlier I argued that modern civilization focuses on the external and disregards the inner world. Moreover, many people, throughout the world, are afraid of the inner realm—they fear the unknown—which I believe partly accounts for the tireless attempts of the Chinese to suppress the highly spiritual tradition and way of life in Tibet. In like manner, Jung arouses the animosity of many who misunderstand and completely distort his concepts and visions, and fail to recognize the depth of his discoveries, which radiate to many fields of inquiry. At times, similarly, even the Dalai Lama's motivation and teachings are grossly distorted and misrepresented. It has been said that Jung was far ahead of his time, which probably explains the difficulty of grasping the profound meaning of his monumental *opus,* his spiritual legacy. In a way, Tibetan Buddhism (together with other spiritual traditions) for centuries has also been ahead of its time. We now realize that much of its cosmology coincides with the findings of modern science.

Jung postulates that there is a common background shared by microphysics and his depth psychology, but it can only be hinted at since in essence it is transcendental.[237] I suspect it is also because we do not yet have the language to describe it. He believes that psyche and matter—the extreme pair of opposites— are not different from each other, since matter produces psyche, and psyche moves matter. He expects that future research will be able to demonstrate the relationship between the mental and the physical. And indeed today the physicist David Bohm has reached the conclusion that "The notion of soma-significance implies that soma (or the physical) and its significance (which is mental) are not in any sense separately existent, but rather they are two aspects of one over-all reality."[238] David Bohm, according to the Tibetan Buddhist master Sogyal Rinpoche, takes a scientific approach to reality with "an understanding of the totality and oneness of existence as an unbroken and seamless whole."[239] This strikingly echoes Jung's statement that synchronistic events point to a profound harmony between all forms of existence."[240]

In another proof of interaction between psyche and matter, medical science has found compelling evidence that distant prayer, meditation, or compassionate thoughts have positive effects on the state of health of patients who are prayed for, even though they are not aware of it.[241]

Both Tibetan Buddhism and Jung's work are very complex, esoteric, and mystical, while at the same time very practical in their basic simplicity—another pair of opposites, elegantly reconciled for our benefit. As Jung suggests, "every endeavor of our human intelligence should be bent to achieving that simplicity where contradictories are reconciled."[242]

Buddha and Jung both focus on the deliverance from suffering in which the mind or psyche plays the essential role, and they apply any method that is healing and works for a particular individual at a particular time. They are not hindered by the dictates of any dogma, doctrine, or psychological theory, although both systems aim toward the development of our consciousness and our full potential, the creative possibilities latent in each of us, on the basis of ethical conduct in all our actions. Jung felt that a religious attitude in life is indispensable for the health of an individual, and he encouraged his patients to follow whatever spiritual path was meaningful to them. Similarly, today the Dalai Lama often begins his teachings by urging listeners to stay with their own religious traditions. What is important, His Holiness tells us, is inner transformation.

There are five billion human beings and in a certain way
I think we need five billion different religions because
there is such a large variety of disposition, natural incli-
nation, temperament, belief, family, and cultural background.[243]

The Dalai Lama rightly recognizes that religious symbols of
a particular culture are essential to the individual if his or her
spiritual quest is to be authentic and not a meaningless imita-
tion. However, Buddhism does not subscribe to a blind accept-
ance of its teachings, even those coming from the Buddha himself.
Lama Yeshe reminds us that a believing mind is a wall that
obscures our clarity and maintains our confusion. We need to be
open, awake, and in a receptive mode to hear the whispers of
the soul, "the news that is always arising out of silence,"[244] from
the depth and height of our unconscious. Therefore, we need
meditation and contemplation so that we can be still and allow
our inner wisdom to speak to us and then integrate it into our
lives. As Jung emphasizes, only direct, immediate experience can
teach the wisdom we hear from teachers or read in books.

In musing over Jung's warning that "the world hangs on a
thin thread and that is the psyche of man," what can we learn
from Tibetan Buddhism and from Jung to apply in our lives as
individuals and help avert global catastrophe? (After all, we
know from historical examples that individuals can and do make
a difference.) From the Tibetans we can learn how to avoid
becoming slaves to afflictive emotions such as anger, hatred, and
revenge, and instead act with mindfulness, skill, and compassion. In Jung's view—and I would take this also to be the responsibility of each one of us—we must begin with the individual,
since the single individual's unconscious is the container of all
destructive forces and at the same time the matrix of wisdom,
inspiration, creativity, and religious experience. To Jung the psyche is both the mother of civilization and its destroyer.[245] We have
the responsibility to choose. Individuals who have achieved a

psychological transformation, or are at least on a journey toward it, positively influence their surroundings without conscious intention. This acts as a positive psychic contagion that has far-reaching, rippling effects.

Let us hear Jung at the beginning of the twentieth century articulating his vision, which could not be more relevant at the dawn of the twenty-first century, and which echoes the essence of Buddhist teachings:

> Too many still look outwards, some believing in the illusion of victory and of victorious power, others in treaties and laws, and others again in the overthrow of the existing order. But still too few look inwards, to their own selves, and still fewer ask themselves whether the ends of human society might not best be served if each man tried to abolish the old order in himself, and to practise in his own person and in his own inward state those precepts, those victories which he preaches at every street-corner, instead of always expecting these things of his fellow men. Every individual needs revolution, inner division, overthrow of the existing order, and renewal, but not by forcing them upon his neighbours under the hypocritical cloak of Christian love or the sense of social responsibility or any of the other beautiful euphemisms for unconscious urges to personal power. Individual self-reflection, return of the individual to the ground of human nature, to his own deepest being with its individual and social destiny—here is the beginning of a cure for that blindness which reigns at the present hour.[246]

In conclusion, I suggest that the most significant and valuable characteristic of both Tibetan Buddhism and Jung's work is that they are forever alive, moving in flux, never static, rigid, or frozen, and for some, always liberating and healing.

Notes

CHAPTER I

1 Walpola Rahula, *What the Buddha Taught* (Bedford: Gordon Fraser, 1959), p. 1.

2 Rahula, op. cit., pp. 45–50.

3 Lama Thubten Yeshe, "Turning the Wheel," in *Wisdom Energy 2* (Ulverston: Wisdom Culture, 1979), p. 24.

4 Edward Conze, *Buddhism* (London: Faber and Faber, 1969), p. 93.

5 Nancy Wilson Ross, *Buddhism: A Way of Life and Thought* (New York: Vintage Books, 1981), p. 44.

6 Gampopa, *The Jewel Ornament of Liberation* (Berkeley: Shambhala, 1971), p. 7.

7 Charles Muses, *East-West Fire: Schopenhauer's Optimism and the Lankavatara Sutra* (London: John Watkins, 1950), p. 45.

8 K. Venkata Ramanan, *Nagarjuna's Philosophy* (New York: Samuel Weiser, 1966), p. 145.

9 Ibid., p. 299.

10 Ibid., p. 297.

11 Tenzin Gyatso, The Fourteenth Dalai Lama, *The Buddhism of Tibet and The Key to the Middle Way* (London: George Allen & Unwin, 1975), pp. 21–22.

12 Lama Thubten Zopa Rinpoche, "The Three Principal Aspects of the Path to Enlightenment,"in Lama Thubten Yeshe and Lama Thubten Zopa Rinpoche, *Wisdom Energy* (Boston: Wisdom Publications, 2000), p. 75.

13 In Zen this is called the "monkey mind," jumping from one place to another.

14 Geshe Ngawang Dhargyey, *Tibetan Tradition of Mental Development* (Dharamsala: Library of Tibetan Works and Archives, 1974), p. 58.

15 It is interesting to note that in a discourse I heard, one Lama equated sin with confusion.

16 Lama Thubten Zopa Rinpoche, op. cit., pp. 84–86.

17 Tenzin Gyatso, op. cit., p. 46.

18 I have often seen and heard psychiatric patients say in group therapy that they forgot about their own troubles, their own miserable lives, as they were in the process of trying to help a fellow patient. Also, in an experimental project I conducted in a psychiatric clinic, showing short art films to schizophrenic or other severely disturbed patients, I was impressed with their positive responses, the enthusiasm and inspiration that these films generated. Many patients told me, even months later, that the weekly viewing of the films had made a significant difference in their dull lives, and some furthermore felt less of a need to rely on medications.

19 Lama Thubten Zopa Rinpoche, op. cit., p. 58.

20 Lama Thubten Yeshe, "Karma and Emptiness," op. cit., p. 52.

21 *Skandhas* in Buddhist teachings are our psychophysical aggregates: our body, feelings, perceptions, impulses and emotions, and basic consciousness.

22 Conze, op. cit., pp. 130–31.

23 The *Lankavatara Sutra,* translated by Daisetz Teitaro Suzuki (London: Routledge & Kegan Paul, 1932), p. 67.

24 Geshe Ngawang Dhargyey, op. cit., p. 29.

25 Dalai Lama, *My Land and My People* (New York: Potala, 1962), p. 241.

26 Geshe Ngawang Dhargyey, op. cit., p. 29.

27 Mircea Eliade, *Yoga, Immortality and Freedom* (Princeton: Princeton University Press, 1970), p. 202.

28 Karl Springer, "Tibetan Buddhism in the West," *The Tibetan Journal,* Vol. 1, no. 3–4 (Autumn 1976), p. 76.

29 This, once again, is very much in the spirit of Buddha who taught different people using different approaches, methods, and philosophies depending on their inclinations, tastes, temperaments, levels of education, and spiritual development.

30 S. B. Dasgupta, *An Introduction to Tantric Buddhism* (Calcutta: University of Calcutta, 1974), p. 54.

31 Ibid., p. 145.

32 Lama Anagarika Govinda, *Foundations of Tibetan Mysticism* (London: Rider & Company, 1959), pp. 94–96

33 Dasgupta, op. cit., p. 145.

34 Ibid., p. 146.

35 "The Vow of Mahamudra," by Garmapa Rinchen Dorje, in C. A. Muses, ed. *Esoteric Teachings of the Tibetan Tantra* (New York: Altai Press, 1961), p. 304.

36 Lama Govinda, op. cit., p. 103.

37 Idem.

38 Ibid., p. 104.

39 Dasgupta, op. cit., p. 188.

40 Ibid., pp. 193–94.

41 Herbert Guenther, *The Tantric View of Life* (Boulder: Shambhala, 1976), p. 37.

42 Quoted in ibid., p. 38.

43 Dasgupta, op. cit., p. 187.

44 Giuseppe Tucci, *The Theory of Practice of the Mandala* (New York: Samuel Weiser, 1970), p. 78.

CHAPTER 2

45 C. G. Jung, *Memories, Dreams, Reflections* (New York: Vintage Books, 1961), pp. 44–45.

46 Jung, op. cit., p. xii.

47 Ibid., p. 222.

48 Ibid., p. 179.

49 Ibid., p. 188.

50 Ibid., p. 194.

51 Ibid., p. 195.

52 Ibid., p. 193. (Italics added.)

53 Ibid., p. 196.

54 Idem.

55 Ibid., p. 199.

56 Idem.

57 Ibid., p. 204.

58 Idem.

59 C. G. Jung, *Two Essays on Analytical Psychology* (Princeton: Princeton University Press, 1966), p. 220.

60 C. G. Jung, *The Archetypes and the Collective Unconscious* (Princeton: Princeton University Press, 1969), p. 44.

61   Ibid., p. 42.

62   Ibid., p. 43.

63   Jung, *Two Essays on Analytical Psychology,* p. 66.

64   Jung, *The Archetypes and the Collective Unconscious,* p. 48.

65   Jung, *Two Essays on Analytical Psychology,* p. 67.

66   Ibid., p. 68.

67   Ibid., p. 238.

68   C. G. Jung, *Aion* (Princeton: Princeton University Press, 1959), p. 63.

69   C. G. Jung, "Answer to Job," in *Psychology and Religion: West and East* (Princeton: Princeton University Press, 1969), p. 468.

70   Jung, *Two Essays on Analytical Psychology,* p. 219.

71   Jung, *The Structure and Dynamics of the Psyche* (Princeton: Princeton University Press, 1969), p. 90.

72   Ibid., p. 91.

73   Russell Lockhart, "Eros in Language, Myth, and Dream," *Quadrant* (Fall 1978), p. 66.

74   Levy-Bruhl's term describing the basic nature of primitive mentality.

75   C. G. Jung, *Psychology and Alchemy* (Princeton: Princeton University Press, 1968), p. 34. "Our gold is not the common gold." It is the gold within each of us.

76   Jung, *Psychology and Alchemy,* p. 244.

77   Ibid., p. 312.

78   Jung, *Aion,* p. 264.

79   C. G. Jung, *Mysterium Coniunctionis* (Princeton: Princeton University Press, 1970), p. 3.

80   Ibid., pp. 106–11.

81   Zen koans perform such a function.

82   Quoted in Ralph Metzner, *Maps of Consciousness* (New York: Macmillan Publishing Co., 1971), pp. 94–95.

83   C. G. Jung, *Alchemical Studies* (Princeton: Princeton University Press, 1967), pp. 237–41.

84   Jung, *Mysterium Coniunctionis,* p. 63.

85   Ibid., pp. 534–40.

86   Ibid., pp. 554–56.

87   Jung, *Memories, Dreams, Reflections,* p. 197.

88   Jung, *The Structure and Dynamics of the Psyche,* p. 520.

89   Ibid., pp. 525–26.

90 Ibid., pp. 421–22.

91 Jung, *Mysterium Coniunctionis*, p. 538.

92 Jung, *Aion*, p. 261.

CHAPTER 3

93 Jung, *Memories, Dreams, Reflections*, p. 124.

94 Jung, *Two Essays on Analytical Psychology*, p. 110.

95 C. G. Jung, *The Practice of Psychotherapy* (Princeton: Princeton University Press, 1966), p. 41.

96 C. G. Jung, "Commentary on the Secret of the Golden Flower," in his *Psychology and the East* (Princeton: Princeton University Press, 1978), p. 18.

97 Jung, *The Practice of Psychotherapy*, pp. 7–8.

98 Jung, *Memories, Dreams, Reflections*, p. 131.

99 Jung, "Commentary on the Secret of the Golden Flower," pp. 18–19.

100 Jung, *The Structure and Dynamics of the Psyche*, p. 89.

101 Janet Dallett, "Active Imagination in Practice," in Murray Stein, ed. *Jungian Analysis* (La Salle: Open Court, 1982), p. 182.

102 Jung, *The Practice of Psychotherapy*, p. 75.

103 Ibid., p. 46.

104 Idem.

105 C. G. Jung, *Psychology and Religion: West and East* (Princeton: Princeton University Press, 1969), p. 334.

106 Jung, *Memories, Dreams, Reflections*, p. 143.

107 Ibid., p. 144.

108 Jung, *The Practice of Psychotherapy*, p. 71.

109 Jung, *Mysterium Coniunctionis*, p. 528.

110 Jung, *Memories, Dreams, Reflections*. p. 145.

111 Jung, *The Practice of Psychotherapy*, p. 108.

112 Ira Progoff, "The Man Who Transforms Consciousness," *Eranos Jahrbuch*, XXXV (1966), pp. 138–39. (Italics added.)

113 Ibid., p. 139.

114 Ibid., pp. 139–40.

115 Anagarika Govinda, *The Psychological Attitude of Early Buddhist Philosophy* (London: Rider & Co., 1961), p. 44.

116 Ibid., p. 39.

117   Herbert Guenther and Chögyam Trungpa, *The Dawn of Tantra* (Boulder: Shambhala, 1975), p. 52.

118   Tucci, op. cit., pp. 72–73.

119   Guenther and Trungpa, op. cit., p. 47.

120   Lama Thubten Yeshe, *Silent Mind, Holy Mind* (Ulverston: Wisdom Culture, 1978), pp. 34–36.

121   Jung, *The Practice of Psychotherapy*, pp. 51–52.

122   Govinda, *Foundations of Tibetan Mysticism*, p. 27.

123   Gampopa, op. cit., pp. 31–32.

124   Lama Thubten Yeshe, "Turning the Wheel," p. 20.

CHAPTER 4

125   C. G. Jung, *Man and His Symbols* (New York: Dell Publishing Co., 1964), p. 88.

126   Govinda, *Foundations of Tibetan Mysticism*, pp. 91–92.

127   Jung, *The Archetypes and the Collective Unconscious*, p. 48.

128   Michael Adams, "The Benzene Uroboros," *Spring* (1981), pp. 149–61.

129   Erich Neumann, *The Great Mother* (Princeton: Princeton University Press, 1963), pp. 332–35.

130   Govinda, *Foundations of Tibetan Mysticism*, p. 192.

131   Ibid., p. 172.

132   C. G. Jung, *Psychological Types* (Princeton: Princeton University Press, 1971), p. 446.

133   Nathan Katz, "Anima and mKha'-'gro-ma: A Critical Comparative Study of Jung and Tibetan Buddhism," *The Tibetan Journal*, Vol. 2, No. 3 (Autumn 1977), pp. 13–43.

134   Jung, *Two Essays on Analytical Psychology*, p. 192.

135   S. K. Ramachandra Rao, *Tibetan Meditation: Theory and Practice* (New Delhi: Arnold-Heineman, 1979) p. 32.

136   Jung, *Aion*, p. 11.

137   Ibid., p. 14.

138   Jung, *Psychology and Alchemy*, p. 13.

139   Jung, *The Archetypes and the Collective Unconscious*, p. 142.

140   Edward Edinger, *Ego and Archetypes* (New York: Penguin Books, 1972), p. 102.

141 Jung, *Psychology and Alchemy,* p. 306.

142 Ibid., p. 313.

143 W. Y. Evans-Wentz, ed. *The Tibetan Book of the Dead* (New York: Galaxy, 1960), p. xxxvi.

144 Francesca Fremantle and Chögyam Trungpa, *The Tibetan Book of the Dead* (Boulder: Shambhala, 1975), p. 1.

145 Ibid., p. 10.

146 Evans-Wentz, op. cit., p. li.

147 Fremantle and Trungpa, op. cit., pp. 5–10.

148 Jung, "Commentary on the Secret of the Golden Flower," p. 30.

149 Anagarika Govinda, *Creative Meditation and Multi-Dimensional Consciousness* (Wheaton: Theosophical Publishing House, 1976), p. 61.

150 C. G. Jung, *The Psychogenesis of Mental Disease* (Princeton: Princeton University Press, 1960), p. 270.

151 Jung, *The Archetypes and the Collective Unconscious,* p. 353.

CHAPTER 5

152 Jung, *The Structure and Dynamics of the Psyche,* p. 256.

153 Ibid., p. 350.

154 Jung, *Mysterium Coniunctionis,* p. 109.

155 Jung, *The Archetypes and the Collective Unconscious,* p. 283.

156 Jung, *The Structure and Dynamics of the Psyche,* p. 361.

157 Jung, *Aion,* p. 165.

158 Jung, *The Practice of Psychotherapy,* pp. 319–20.

159 Jung, *Psychological Types,* pp. 449–50.

160 Jung, *Psychology and Alchemy,* p. 137.

161 Jung, *Mysterium Coniunctionis,* p. 197.

162 Jung, *The Structure and Dynamics of the Psyche,* p. 349.

163 Jung, Ibid., p. 185.

164 Jung, *The Archetypes and the Collective Unconscious,* p. 279.

165 Jung, *The Practice of Psychotherapy,* p. 34.

166 Ibid., p. 192.

167 Govinda, *Foundations of Tibetan Mysticism,* pp. 71–77.

168   Govinda, *Creative Meditation and Multi-Dimensional Consciousness,*
      p. 30.

169   Ibid., p. 31.

170   *The Lankavatara Sutra,* p. 48.

171   C. G. Jung, "Septem Sermones ad Mortuos," in his *Memories,*
      Dreams, Reflections, p. 379.

172   *Pleroma* is the Greek word for "plenitude."

173   Jung, "Septem Sermones ad Mortuos," p. 379.

174   Ibid., p. 382.

175   Jung, *Memories, Dreams, Reflections,* p. 269.

176   Govinda, *Foundations of Tibetan Mysticism,* p. 77.

177   Govinda, *Creative Meditation and Multi-Dimensional Consciousness,*
      p. 105.

178   Fritjof Capra, *The Tao of Physics* (Boulder: Shambhala, 1970), p. 99.

179   Quoted in Beatrice Suzuki, *Impressions of Mahayana Buddhism*
      (Kyoto: Eastern Buddhist Society, 1940), p. 48.

180   Jung, *The Practice of Psychotherapy,* p. 312.

181   Jung, *Two Essays on Analytical Psychology,* pp. 75–76.

182   Ibid., p. 75.

183   Ibid., p. 205.

184   Jung, *The Archetypes and the Collective Unconscious,* p. 382.

185   Jung, *Psychological Types,* p. 453.

186   Ramanan, op. cit., p. 50.

187   Ibid., p. 258.

188   Ibid., p. 329.

189   C. G. Jung, "Foreword to Suzuki's Introduction to Zen Buddhism,"
      in his *Psychology and the East,* p. 154.

190   Govinda, *Creative Meditation and Multi-Dimensional Consciousness,*
      pp. 48–49.

191   Jung, *The Structure and Dynamics of the Psyche,* p. 351.

192   C. G. Jung, *Letters* (Princeton: Princeton University Press, 1973), vol.
      1, p. 236.

193   Ibid., vol. 2, p. 248.

194   Jung, *Man and His Symbols,* p. 81.

195   Jung, *Aion,* p. 33.

196   Dhargyey, op. cit., p. 92.

197   Jung, *The Practice of Psychotherapy,* pp. 7–8.

198   C. G. Jung, *Psychological Analysis of Nietzsche's Zarathustra,* vol. 3 (Winter 1935), p. 23.

199   Ibid., p. 4.

200   Jung, *Aion,* p. 13.

201   Govinda, *Creative Meditation and Multi-Dimensional Consciousness,* p. 141.

202   Miguel Serrano, *C. G. Jung and Hermann Hesse; A Record of Two Friendships* (New York: Schocken Books, 1960), p. 88.

203   Jung, *Letters,* vol. 2, p. 314.

204   Idem.

205   Jung, "Commentary on *The Secret of the Golden Flower,*" p. 56.

206   Jung, *Alchemical Studies,* pp. 59–64.

207   Jung, *The Practice of Psychotherapy,* p. 81.

208   Jung, "Psychological Commentary on *The Tibetan Book of Great Liberation,*" p. 111.

209   Jung, "Commentary on *The Secret of the Golden Flower,*" p. 13.

210   Idem.

211   Jung, "Psychological Commentary on *The Tibetan Book of Great Liberation,*" p. 134.

212   Jung, *Psychology and Alchemy,* pp. 99–101.

213   Ibid., p. 125.

214   Ibid., pp. 132–33.

215   Ira Progoff, *The Cloud of Unknowing* (New York: Dell Publishing Co, 1950), pp. 23–38.

216   Elaine Pagels, *The Gnostic Gospels* (New York: Vintage Books, 1979), pp. xx–xxi.

217   Ibid., pp. 149–61.

218   Quoted in Pagels, op. cit., p. 161. (Italics added.)

219   Quoted in Pagels, op. cit., p. 155.

220   Jung, "Psychological Commentary on *The Tibetan Book of Great Liberation,*" p. 112.

221   Jung, *The Archetypes and the Collective Unconscious,* p. 224.

222   Guenther and Trungpa, op. cit., p. 89.

223   Erich Neumann, *The Origins and History of Consciousness* (Princeton: Princeton University Press, 1954), p. 322.

224   Geshe Rabten and Geshe Ngawang Dhargyey, *Advice from a Spiritual Friend* (London: Wisdom Publications, 1984), p. 65.

225 Ibid., pp. 65–66.

226 Jung, *The Undiscovered Self* (New York: The New American Library, 1959), p. 123.

227 Jung, *Two Essays on Analytical Psychology,* p. 226.

228 Jung, *The Undiscovered Self,* pp. 117–18.

229 Jung, "Psychological Commentary on *The Tibetan Book of Great Liberation,*" p. 135.

EPILOGUE

230 Jung, *Aion,* p. 70.

231 Jung, *Mysterium Coniunctionis,* pp. 163–64.

232 Jung, *Letters,* vol. 1, p. 247.

233 Ibid, p. 236.

234 Jung, *Psychology and the East,* p. 210.

235 Lama Yeshe, *Introduction to Tantra: A Vision of Totality* (London: Wisdom Publications, 1987), pp. 88–89.

236 C. G. Jung, *The Spirit in Man, Art, and Literature* (????), p. 54.

237 Jung, *Mysterium Coniunctionis,* p. 538.

238 Sogyal Rinpoche, *The Tibetan Book of Living and Dying* (San Francisco: Harper San Francisco, 1992), p. 353.

239 Ibid.

240 Jung, *Aion,* p. 261.

241 Larry Dossey, *Reinventing Medicine: Beyond Mind-Body to a New Era of Healing* (San Francisco: Harper San Francisco, 1999), p. ???.

242 Jung, *The Practice of Psychotherapy,* p. 320.

243 Tenzin Gyatso, the Fourteenth Dalai Lama, and Howard Cutler, *The Art of Happiness* (New York: Riverhead Books, 1998), p. 294.

244 Rainer Maria Rilke, *Duino Elegies,* quoted in Sogyal Rinpoche, op. cit., p. 81.

245 Jung, *The Archetypes of the Collective Unconscious,* p. 116.

246 Jung, *Two Essays on Analytical Psychology,* p. 5.

Glossary

BUDDHISM

Unless indicated otherwise, all words are Sanskrit.

alaya-vijnana "storehouse consciousness," the source of all consciousness in a person, according to the Chittamatra school of Buddhist tenets

arhat one who has attained complete liberation from suffering, has attained nirvana

Avalokiteshvara the buddha of compassion

bardo the state between death and rebirth

bodhichitta the enlightened motive or attitude possessed by bodhisattvas: the desire to become a buddha in order to benefit all beings

bodhisattva an enlightenment-bound being

buddha a fully enlightened being; one who has overcome all negativities and completed all good qualities

dakini (Tibetan: *khandroma*) a symbolic being in female form who embodies bliss and wisdom and acts as a spiritual helper

Dharma spiritual teachings; the doctrine of the Buddha; universal law

enlightenment the state of being a buddha, when all duality is transcended into absolute unity; the eradication of all negative states of mind and accumulation of all positive qualities

Hinayana early school of Buddhism, southern Buddhism, of which Theravada is the only surviving system

karma the law of cause and effect; the consequences of our thoughts, speech, and actions in this and future lives

karuna compassion

Mahayana later schools of Buddhism that espouse the bodhisattva ideal; northern Buddhism

Manjushri the buddha of wisdom

mantra sacred word, auditory symbol

mudra ritual symbolic gesture

nirvana the state beyond suffering; freedom from karma and delusion and repeated rebirth in samsara

padma lotus blossom; the symbol of spiritual unfoldment

prajna supreme knowledge and intuitive, liberating wisdom; female principle

sadhana spiritual exercise

samadhi a deep state of undisturbed single-pointed concentration

samsara cyclic existence; the cycle of continuous, uncontrolled rebirth into the various realms of existence; continuous mental and physical suffering

satori (Japanese) in Zen Buddhism another name for enlightenment

shunyata emptiness, voidness; all phenomena are said to be empty of inherent existence, or existence from their own side; the flip side of the interdependence of all phenomena

skandhas a human being's psychophysical aggregates: body, feelings, perceptions, impulses and emotions, basic consciousness

tangka (Tibetan) religious painting, usually executed on cloth and framed in brocade

tantra the esoteric teachings of Buddha that lead quickly to enlightenment; special methods and practices for quickly attaining enlightenment; also called *Vajrayana*

Tao (Chinese) eternal way of the cosmic order

Tara a feminine aspect of buddha mind

upaya method; male principle

vajra (Tibetan: *dorje*) diamond sceptre, symbol of indestructibility; the male principle of action

Vajrayana the "diamond vehicle" to enlightenment, part of the Mahayana; tantric school of Buddhism

Vajrayogini a dakini of the highest rank, depicted in brilliant red color and surrounded by a halo of flames

yidam (Tibetan) a male or female deity, or buddha, invoked in certain tantric meditation practices

JUNG

anima the female aspect of the male psyche

anima mundi the Soul of the World

archetypes contents of the collective unconscious; primordial images and patterns of symbol formation that recur throughout humankind

collective unconscious the portion of the psyche whose unconscious contents are hereditary and belonging to humanity in general; by contrast the personal unconscious comprises personal experiences that have been repressed and forgotten

ego a complex of ideas that constitutes the center of one's field of consciousness and appears to possess a high degree of continuity and identity

eros the principle of relatedness

individuation the process of the integration of the personality; the quest for meaning

mandala a Sanskrit word for circle; a pattern of symbolic squares and circles

Philemon Jung's fantasy image of an old man whom he called Philemon, and who represented superior insight; to Jung he was like a guru

pleroma a Greek word for plenitude

psyche the totality of all psychic processes, conscious and unconscious

Self the center of personality, the symbol of wholeness, the principle of orientation and meaning; the culmination of the psychic development

synchronicity acausal connecting principle; a meaningful coincidence when an inner and outer event come together

transcendent function a complex function that in the process of individuation facilitates a transition from one attitude to another

unus mundus one world

Bibliography

Adams, Michael. "The Benzene Uroboros." *Spring* (1981): 149–61.

Adler, Gerhard. *The Living Symbol.* Princeton: Princeton University Press, 1961.

Anderson, Walt. *Open Secrets: A Western Guide to Tibetan Buddhism.* New York: Penguin Books, 1980.

Arguelles, Jose and Miriam. *Mandala.* Boston: Shambala, 1985.

Arnold, Paul. *Avec les Lamas Tibétains.* Paris: Fayard, 1970.

Avalon, Arthur. *The Serpent Power.* Madras: Ganesh & Co., 1950.

Baynes, H. G. *Mythology of the Soul.* London: Methuen Co., 1940.

Bishop, Peter. "Archetypal Topography." *Spring* (1981): 67–76.

Blofeld, John. *Beyond the Gods.* New York: E. P. Dutton, 1974.

———. *The Tantric Mysticism of Tibet.* New York: E. P. Dutton, 1970.

Bolen, Jean. *The Tao of Psychology.* San Francisco: Harper & Row, 1979.

Byles, Marie. "Vipassana Meditation and Psychologist Jung." *The Maha Bodhi,* vol. 68 (Dec. 1960): 362–66.

Capra, Fritjof. *The Tao of Physics.* Boulder: Shambhala, 1975.

Chang, C. C. Chang. *Teachings of Tibetan Yoga.* Secaucus: The Citadel Press, 1963.

Chang, Chung-yuan. *Creativity and Taoism.* New York: Harper & Row, 1963.

Chodron, Thubten. *What Color Is Your Mind?* Ithaca: Snow Lion, 1993.

Conze, Edward. *Buddhism.* London: Faber and Faber, 1963.

Coukoulis, Peter. *Guru, Psychotherapist, and Self.* Marina del Rey: DeVorss & Co., 1976.

Coward, Harold. *Jung and Eastern Thought.* Albany: State University of New York, 1985.

Dagyab, Londen Sherap Rinpoche. *Buddhist Symbols in Tibetan Culture.* Boston: Wisdom Publications, 1995.

Dasgupta, Shashi. *An Introduction to Tantric Buddhism.* Calcutta: University of Calcutta, 1974.

David-Neel, Alexandra. *The Secret Oral Teachings in Tibetan Buddhist Sects*. San Francisco: City Lights Books, 1967.

Dhargyey, Geshe Ngawang. *Tibetan Tradition of Mental Development*. Dharamsala: Library of Tibetan Works and Archives, 1974.

Dossey, Larry. *Reinventing Medicine: Beyond Mind-Body to a New Era of Healing*. San Francisco: Harper San Francisco, 1999.

Edinger, Edward. *Ego and Archetype*. New York: Penguin Books, 1973.

———. "Psychotherapy and Alchemy." *Quadrant* (Summer 1978–Spring 1980).

Eliade, Mircea. *Yoga, Immortality and Freedom*. Princeton: Princeton University Press, 1969.

Evans-Wentz, W. Y., ed. *The Tibetan Book of the Dead*. New York: Galaxy, 1960.

———. *The Tibetan Book of the Great Liberation*. London: Oxford University Press, 1968.

Fierz, Heinrich. "The Lambspring Figures." *The Well-Tended Tree*, edited by Hilda Kirsh. New York: G. P. Putnam, 1971.

Fremantle, Francesca, and Chögyam Trungpa. *The Tibetan Book of the Dead*. Boulder: Shambhala, 1975.

Gampopa. *The Jewel Ornament of Liberation*. Berkeley: Shambala, 1971.

Goleman, Daniel. "On the Significance of Buddhist Psychology for the West." *The Tibetan Journal*, vol. 1, no. 2 (April–June 1976): 37–42.

Goswani, Amit. *The Self-Aware Universe: How Consciousness Creates the Material World*. New York: G. P. Putnam, 1993.

———. *Visionary Window: A Quantum Physicist's Guide to Enlightenment*. Wheaton: Quest Books, 2001.

Govinda Lama Anagarika. *Creative Meditation and Multi-Dimensional Consciousness*. Wheaton: Theosophical Publishing House, 1976.

———. *Foundations of Tibetan Mysticism*. York Beach: Samuel Weiser, 1969.

———. *The Psychological Attitude of Early Buddhist Philosophy*. London: Rider & Co., 1961.

Guenther, Herbert. *The Tantric View of Life*. Boulder: Shambhala, 1976.

———. *Tibetan Buddhism in Western Perspective*. Emeryville: Dharma Publishing, 1977.

Guenther, Herbert, and Chögyam Trungpa. *The Dawn of Tantra*. Boulder: Shambhala, 1975.

Guenther, Herbert, and Leslie Kawamura, trans. *Mind in Buddhist Psychology*. Emeryville: Dharma Publishing, 1975.

Gyatso, Tenzin, The Fourteenth Dalai Lama. *The Buddhism of Tibet and The Key to the Middle Way.* London: George Allen and Unwin, 1975.

————. *The Good Heart: A Buddhist Perspective on the Teachings of Jesus.* Boston: Wisdom Publications, 1996.

————. *A Human Approach to World Peace.* London: Wisdom Publications, 1984.

————. *My Land and My People.* New York: Potala Corporation, 1977.

————. *Opening the Eye of New Awareness.* Translated and introduced by Donald S. Lopez, Jr. with Jeffery Hopkins. Boston: Wisdom Publications, 1984, 1999.

Gyatso, Tenzin, et al. *Mind Science: An East-West Dialogue.* Boston: Wisdom Publications, 1991.

Gyatso, Tenzin, and Howard C. Cutler. *The Art of Happiness: A Handbook for Living.* New York: Riverhead Books, 1998.

Hesse, Herman. *Journey to the East.* Translated by Hilda Rosner. London: P. Owen, 1956.

————. *Siddhartha.* New York: New Directions, 1951.

Hillman, James. "Anima." *Spring* (1973).

————. "Further Notes on Images." *Spring* (1978).

————. "Inquiry into an Image." *Spring* (1977).

————. "Therapeutic Value of Alchemical Language." *Dragonflies* (Fall 1978).

Hopkins, Jeffrey. *The Tantric Distinction.* Boston: Wisdom Publications, 1984, 1999.

Houston, Gary. "Mandalas: Ritual and Functional." *The Tibetan Journal,* vol. 1 no. 2 (Apr./June 1976): 47–58.

Humphreys, Christmas. *The Buddhist Way of Life.* London: George Allen and Unwin, 1980.

————. *Studies in the Middle Way.* London: George Allen and Unwin, 1959.

Jacobi, Jolande. *The Psychology of C. G. Jung.* New Haven: Yale University Press, 1973.

Jaffe, Aniela, ed. *C. G. Jung: Word and Image.* Princeton: Princeton University Press, 1979.

Jarrett, James. "Schopenhauer and Jung." *Spring* (1981).

Johnson, Robert. *Inner Work.* San Francisco: Harper & Row, 1986.

Johnston, William. *Silent Music.* New York: Harper & Row, 1974.

Jung, Carl Gustav. *Aion.* Princeton: Princeton University Press, 1979.

————. *Alchemical Studies.* Princeton: Princeton University Press, 1967.

———. *Analytical Psychology.* New York: Vintage Books, 1970.

———. "Answer to Job." In *Psychology and Religion: West and East.* Princeton: Princeton University Press, 1969.

———. *The Archetypes and the Collective Unconscious.* Princeton: Princeton University Press, 1969.

———. *C. G. Jung Speaking: Interviews and Encounters.* Edited by William McGuire and R. F. C. Hull. Princeton: Princeton University Press, 1971.

———. *The Development of Personality.* Princeton: Princeton University Press, 1981.

———. *Letters.* Vol. 1: 1906–1950. Princeton: Princeton University Press, 1973. Vol. 2: 1951–1961. Princeton: Princeton University Press, 1975.

———. *Man and His Symbols.* New York: Dell Publishing Co., 1968.

———. *Memories, Dreams, Reflections.* New York: Vintage Books, 1961.

———. *Mysterium Coniunctionis.* Princeton: Princeton University Press, 1977.

———. *The Practice of Psychotherapy.* Princeton: Princeton University Press, 1966.

———. "Psychological Commentary on Kundalini Yoga." *Spring* (1975 and 1976).

———. *Psychological Types.* Princeton: Princeton University Press, 1971.

———. *Psychology and Alchemy.* Princeton: Princeton University Press, 1980.

———. *Psychology and the East.* Princeton: Princeton University Press, 1978.

———. "Septem Sermones ad Mortuos." In *Memories, Dreams, Reflections,* Appendix V: 378–90.

———. *The Spirit in Man, Art, and Literature.* Princeton: Princeton University Press, 1966.

———. *The Structure and Dynamics of the Psyche.* Princeton: Princeton University Press, 1969.

———. *Two Essays on Analytical Psychology.* Princeton: Princeton University Press, 1972.

———. *The Undiscovered Self.* New York: The New American Library, 1959.

Jung, Carl Gustav, and Shin-ichi Hisamatsu. "On the Unconscious, the Self and Therapy."*Psychologia,* vol. 11 (1968): 25–32.

Katz, Nathan. "Anima and mKha'-'gro-ma: A Critical Comparative Study of Jung and Tibetan Buddhism." *The Tibetan Journal,* vol. 2, no. 3 (Autumn 1977): 13–43.

Kazantzakis, Nikos. *The Saviors of God.* New York: Simon and Schuster, 1969.

Lauf, Detlef. *Secret Doctrines of the Tibetan Books of the Dead.* Boulder: Shambhala, 1977.

———. *Secret Revelation of Tibetan Thangkas.* Freiburg im Breisgau: Aurum Verlag, 1976.

Lockhart, Russell. "Eros in Language, Myth, and Dream." *Quadrant* (Fall 1978): 41–68.

———. "Psyche in Hiding." *Quadrant* (Spring, 1980).

———. *Psyche Speaks.* Wilmette: Chiron Publications, 1987.

McDonald, Kathleen. *How to Meditate.* Boston: Wisdom Publications, 1984.

Meckel, Daniel, and Robert Moore, eds. *Self and Liberation: The Jung-Buddhism Dialogue.* New York: Paulist Press, 1992.

Merton, Thomas. *The Asian Journal of Thomas Merton.* New York: New Directions, 1975.

Metzner, Ralph. *Maps of Consciousness.* New York: Macmillan Publishing Co., 1971.

Mitchell, Edgar. *The Ways of the Explorer: An Apollo Astronaut's Journey Through the Material and Mystical Worlds.* New York: G. P. Putnam, 1996.

Miyuki, Mokusan. "A Jungian Approach to the Pure Land Practice." Paper presented at the Sixth Annual Conference of Jungian Analysts, Asilomar, California, March 1979.

Murti, T. R. V. *The Central Philosophy of Buddhism.* London: George Allen & Unwin, 1955.

Muses, Charles. *East-West Fire: Schopenhauer's Optimism and The Lankavatara Sutra.* London: John Watkins, 1955.

———, ed. *Esoteric Teachings of the Tibetan Tantra.* New York: Altai Press, 1961.

Neumann, Erich. *The Great Mother.* Princeton: Princeton University Press, 1963.

———. *The Origins and History of Consciousness.* Princeton: Princeton University Press, 1954.

Nhat Hanh, Thich. *Living Buddha, Living Christ.* New York: Riverside Books, 1995.

———. *Peace Is Every Step.* New York: Bantam Books, 1991.

Norby, Thinley. *Welcoming Flowers: An Answer to the Pope's Criticism of Buddhism.* New York: Jewel Publishing House, 1997.

Pagels, Elaine. *The Gnostic Gospels.* New York: Vintage Books, 1979.

Perry, John. *The Far Side of Madness.* Englewood Cliffs: Prentice-Hall, 1974.

———. *Roots of Renewal in Myth and Madness.* San Francisco: Jossey-Bass, 1976.

Progoff, Ira. *The Cloud of Unknowing.* New York: Dell Publishing Co., 1957.

———. *The Death and Rebirth of Psychology.* New York: The Julian Press, 1959.

———. *Depth Psychology and Modern Man.* New York: The Julian Press, 1956.

———. *Jung's Psychology and Its Social Meaning.* New York: The Julian Press, 1969.

———. *Jung's Synchronicity and Human Destiny.* New York: The Julian Press, 1973.

——— "The Man Who Transforms Consciousness." *Eranos Jahrbuch,* vol. xxxv (1966): 99–144.

———. *The Symbolic and the Real.* New York: The Julian Press, 1963.

Rabten, Geshe, and Geshe Ngawang Dhargyey. *Advice from a Spiritual Friend.* Boston: Wisdom Publications, 1996.

Rahula, Walpola. *What the Buddha Taught.* Bedford: Gordon Fraser, 1959.

Ramanan, K. Venkata. *Nagarjuna's Philosophy.* New York: Samuel Weiser, 1966.

Rao, S. K. Ramachandra. *Tibetan Meditation: Theory and Practice.* New Delhi: Arnold-Heinemann, 1979.

Ravindra, Ravi. *Science and Spirit.* New York: Paragon House, 1991.

Ross, Nancy Wilson. *Buddhism: A Way of Life and Thought.* New York: Vintage Books, 1981.

———. *Three Ways of Asian Wisdom.* New York: Simon and Schuster, 1968.

Russell, Peter. *From Science to God.* (Pre-publication edition, 2000).

Santideva, Acharya. *A Guide to the Bodhisattva's Way of Life.* Dharamsala: Library of Tibetan Works & Archives, 1979.

Serrano, Miguel. *C. G. Jung and Hermann Hesse: A Record of Two Friendships.* New York: Schocken Books, 1966.

Snellgrove, D. L. *The Hevajra Tantra.* London: Oxford University, 1959.

Sogyal Rinpoche. *The Tibetan Book of Living and Dying.* San Francisco: Harper San Francisco, 1992.

Springer, Karl. "Tibetan Buddhism in the West." *The Tibetan Journal,* vol. 1, no. 3 (Autumn 1976): 75–80.

Stein, Murray. *Jungian Analysis*. La Salle: Open Court, 1982.

Suzuki, Beatrice. *Impressions of Mahayana Buddhism*. Kyoto: Eastern Buddhist Society, 1940.

Suzuki, Daisez T. *Outlines of Mahayana Buddhism*. New York: Schocken Books, 1963.

————, trans. *The Lankavatara Sutra*. London: Routledge & Kegan Paul, 1932.

Trungpa, Chögyam. "The Tibetan Heritage of Buddhist Art." *The Tibetan Journal*, vol. 1, no. 2 (Apr./June 1976): 5–9.

Tucci, Guiseppe. *The Theory and Practice of the Mandala*. New York: Samuel Weiser, 1970.

Valle, Ronald, and Rolf von Eckartsberg, eds., *The Metaphors of Consciousness*. New York: Plenum Press, 1981.

Van der Post, Laurens. *Jung and the Story of Our Time*. New York: Pantheon Books, 1975.

Vasavada, Arwind. "Free-Less Practice and Soul Work." In Russell Lockhart et al. *Soul and Money*. Dallas: Spring Publications, 1982.

Von Franz, Marie-Louise. *C. G. Jung: His Myth in Our Time*. Boston: Little, Brown and Co., 1975.

————. *Psyche and Matter*. Boston: Shambala, 1992.

Walsh, Roger, and Frances Vaughan, eds. *Paths Beyond Ego: The Transpersonal Vision*. New York: Jeremy Tarcher, 1993.

Wilber, Ken. *The Spectrum of Consciousness*. Wheaton: The Theosophical Publishing House, 1982.

Yeshe, Lama Thubten. *Introduction to Tantra*. Boston: Wisdom Publications, 2001.

————. *Silent Mind, Holy Mind*. Ulverston: Wisdom Culture, 1978.

————. *The Tantric Path of Purification*. Boston: Wisdom Publications, 1995.

Yeshe, Lama Thubten, et al. *Wisdom Energy 2*. Ulverston: Wisdom Culture, 1979.

Yeshe, Lama Thubten, and Lama Thubten Zopa Rinpoche. *Wisdom Energy*. Boston: Wisdom Publications, 2000.

Zopa, Lama Thubten Rinpoche. *The Door to Satisfaction*. Boston: Wisdom Publications, 1994.

————. *Transforming Problems into Happiness*. Boston: Wisdom Publications, 2001.

Index

About the Author

Radmila Moacanin was born in Belgrade, Yugoslavia. She studied in Geneva, New York, and Los Angeles, and earned a diploma in Languages, a master's degree in United Nations and World Affairs, a master's degree in social service, and a Ph.D. in psychology. She was a Fulbright scholar in Italy.

Dr. Moacanin has worked at the Permanent Mission of Burma to the United Nations, at the New York University Medical Center, and at the University of Southern California Medical Center. She has served as consultant in the National Intensive Journal Program, and has been a visiting lecturer at the School of Psychology in Moscow. At present Radmila Moacanin lives in Los Angeles and works as a psychotherapist, an adjunct professor at the San Diego University for Integrative Studies, and a conductor of Writing Meditation retreats in California. She has traveled extensively throughout the world and speaks six languages. For over three decades the author has been a student of both of Zen and Tibetan Buddhism.

Wisdom Publications

Wisdom Publications, a not-for-profit publisher, is dedicated to making available authentic Buddhist works for the benefit of all. We publish translations of the sutras and tantras, commentaries and teachings of past and contemporary Buddhist masters, and original works by the world's leading Buddhist scholars. We publish our titles with an appreciation of Buddhism as a living philosophy and with a special commitment to preserve and transmit important works from all the major Buddhist traditions.

To learn more about Wisdom, or to browse books online, visit our website at wisdompubs.org. You may request a copy of our mail-order catalog online or by writing to:

Wisdom Publications
199 Elm Street
Somerville, Massachusetts 02144 USA
Telephone: (617) 776-7416
Fax: (617) 776-7841
Email: info@wisdompubs.org
www.wisdompubs.org

THE WISDOM TRUST

As a not-for-profit publisher, Wisdom is dedicated to the publication of fine Dharma books for the benefit of all sentient beings and dependent upon the kindness and generosity of sponsors in order to do so. If you would like to make a donation to Wisdom, please do so through our Somerville office. If you would like to sponsor the publication of a book, please write or email us at the address above.

Thank you.

Wisdom is a nonprofit, charitable 501(c)(3) organization affiliated with the Foundation for the Preservation of the Mahayana Tradition (FPMT).